YOU, THE GIRL WHO READS THIS

ERASTO PHILIPPE

Published by Xenoloop Publishing House

under the imprint Xenoloop Voices.

ISBN (Paperback): 978-81-988896-6-9
ISBN (eBook): 978-81-988896-6-8

Publisher contact: editor@xenoloop.in

DEDICATION

To all the wonderful women, those I met, those I did not, and those who left their legacies to us.
And, most importantly, to you, the girl who reads this: this book is dedicated.

CONTENTS

ACKNOWLEDGMENTS

This book was not written in isolation. It was written in the space between conversations, after listening, learning, and witnessing the strength that women show in ways the world rarely applauds.

First, I thank my mother and my family. The love, discipline, and values I grew up with became the foundation from which these letters were possible. I thank my sisters for teaching me, often without words, what it means to stand your ground with grace.

To the women who trusted me with their stories, friends, colleagues, students, mentors, and strangers who became lessons, I carry your courage with respect. Some moments in this book are inspired by real people and real experiences. Where details have been altered, it was done to protect privacy, not to dilute truth.

To the mentors and managers who shaped my principles, thank you for showing me that strength can be gentle, and leadership can be humane.

To the readers, thank you for giving this book your time. If even one chapter feels like a hand on your shoulder, then these pages have done what they were meant to do.

Finally, my gratitude to Xenoloop Publishing House and the Xenoloop Voices imprint for believing in a book built from letters, simple words, written with the hope of offering companionship and courage.

PREFACE

This book began as a sentence I could not stop writing:

"You, the girl who reads this..."

It felt like a doorway. Not into one story, but into many. Because there is not one kind of woman. There are women who grieve, and women who rebuild. Women who carry families, women who carry dreams, women who carry both. Women who are praised too late, questioned too soon, and expected to endure without asking for anything in return.

What follows is written as letters, not speeches, not lectures, not instructions. Letters are different. A letter does not stand above you. It sits beside you. It does not try to fix you; it tries to stay with you.

Each chapter in Part I is a direct address to a woman at a threshold: grief, responsibility, divorce, motherhood, work, sport, identity, dignity, ageing, moments when life feels heavy and the world becomes loud with opinions. These letters are meant to be plain, memorable, and kind. Read them in order if you want a journey, or open anywhere when you need a voice that does not rush you.

The emotional arc moves through three quiet movements: Becoming, Belonging, Legacy. Becoming is where we first learn what we are made of. Belonging is where we learn boundaries, love, and self-respect. Legacy is where we begin to understand that our lives mean something, not because they were perfect, but because we kept going.

In Part II, the letters widen into stories: snapshots of the women who made this book possible. They are not written to expose anyone, but to honor what is often unseen, the silent battles, the steady faces, the courage that looks ordinary from the outside.

If you are the girl who reads this, I hope you feel recognized here. If you are the man who reads this, I hope you learn to see more clearly.
And if you are anyone who has been loved by a woman, I hope this book reminds you to say the words while there is still time: Thank you. I notice. You matter.

You may begin now.

PART I – LETTERS FOR YOU, THE GIRL WHO READS THIS

These pages are written as letters, not speeches, not instructions, and never a judgement. They are small, steady messages meant to find you in real life: in the middle of grief, in the middle of responsibility, in the middle of starting over, in the middle of becoming someone you did not know you could be. Read them in order if you want a journey, or open anywhere when you need a hand to hold, because the point is not perfection; it's companionship. And every time a chapter begins, "You, the girl who reads this," it is not a line on paper, it is a reminder that you are seen, you are surviving, and you are allowed to keep going, one brave step at a time.

1. THE GOOD SISTER

You, the girl who reads this, sisters like you are the quiet strength behind many families.

Truth be told, the luckiest of brothers is the brother who has a sister as his sibling. A sister is not only a sibling; she is often a second mother, a counsellor, a peacekeeper, the mediator when there is a fight, the one who notices what everyone else misses. Yet being a sister comes with its own weight. And yes, it hurts when your brother seems to get more freedom. It can feel unfair, even when parents repeat the same line: "These restrictions are for your own good."

Here is what you need to remember: your discipline will become your advantage. Your obedience to your parents will become your foundation for a strong relationship with them. While others chase temporary excitement, you are building skills, stability, and a deeper bond with the parents who raised you. You are learning patience, responsibility, and resilience, qualities that will carry you farther than "freedom" ever will.

So, to you, I say: your brother may get more freedom today, but you are gaining something bigger, strength, focus, your parents' deep love, and a future that will open widely for you.

2. *THE FRIEND WHO TEACHES*

You, the girl who reads this, a friend like you who dedicates her time to helping her friends learn and still manages to get good grades herself, is a rare blessing.

A teacher can only do so much within a set timetable. So, life's best gift to people who learn more slowly is an unofficial teacher like you, a friend who teaches, explains, revises, repeats, and encourages when someone is ready to give up.

One day, your friends will look back and say, "We celebrated our teachers on Teachers' Day, but we also had an unofficial one: a friend who taught us what the classroom couldn't, who stayed behind for us even when the bell rang, and who didn't give up on us when we were ready to give up." And when they say that, the only person they'll think of will be you!

Your friends are blessed to have you, and thanks to your little knowledge transfers, their future will be bright.

3. THE BRIDE-TO-BE

You, the girl who reads this, first, congratulations on your upcoming wedding. May you have the most beautiful wedding you deserve and dream of.

A life-changing event, such as a wedding, can be nerve-racking. But it is normal to feel nervous. It is normal to get cold feet and hear whispers of, "What if it goes wrong?"

But my dear friend, what if it goes right?

You are not alone. You never will be. The same family that held you through your first steps, school, college, life will hold you now and forever. Marriage changes your address, not your relationship with your parents. The bond between parents and a daughter is too strong to fade just because she gets married and moves to a new home. So, to you, I say this: breathe. All good things can be scary at first. You were loved in your old home; you will be loved in your new one, too.

4. THE NEW MOTHER

You, the girl who reads this, as the saying goes, childbirth is a mother's rebirth. The sacrifices, the hard work, and the resilience you showed through pregnancy and labor, and the way you've begun to heal in the postpartum period, are nothing short of extraordinary.

Motherhood, with its responsibility can press on the chest. Anxiety happens; panic visits; doubt creeps in, but never mistake any of it for weakness. If someone asked me to show both overwhelming fear and the strong will to fight, I would point them to a mother's eyes, your eyes.

Dear friend, new beginnings are always hard. Bringing your baby into the world was hard, yet you did it. Raising a baby well will be hard, too, and yet, you will do that, too. You knew labor would test you, and still it was your easiest "yes" for your baby's sake. So, when worry swells, remember: you will do anything and everything for a good life for your baby.

You can worry later. These early days are tender and bright. Savor them, babies grow fast. Trust your instincts; you will learn your child like a language. Your parents raised you with care and love; after all, you are their girl. You will pour the same love, if not more, into your own.

5. THE NEWLYWED

You, the girl who reads this, the world should understand that no newlywed can instantly feel at home in her in-laws' house. Even the most demanding professions on earth are not asked to adapt to change as quickly as a newlywed is expected to in her new home.

Being told overnight to stop and start again: new relationship in a new house with new people, new relatives, a new neighborhood, new rules and norms, enough to shake even the most confidents' confidence.

You have heard the stories, even seen a few with your own eyes, freedoms taken, lines crossed, quarrels that turn into cold wars, fights that split families. Everything whispers that it might happen to you, too.

But fear not. Not everyone's path is the same. This life is new, yes, but trust your record. You have done "new" before: new friend circles, new schools and colleges, new teams and workplaces, new places and new challenges. You found your footing then; you will find it now, too. Even when you do not know what to do, you will figure something out. Many fine women, far less educated and experienced than you, have stood where you stand now and gone on to build happy families; you can, too.

What your parents gave you, your education, skills, and steadiness, does not vanish. Your old friends and relatives do not cease to exist; in this new life, more are added. The mind sometimes tricks us into believing the old was always best, but was it? There was always good mixed with bad then, too. This season will be the same: some bad, much good. Keep the good; let the rest pass.

It takes time for a house to soften into a home. If you feel like you are starting from zero, so be it, you will build. What feels like a restart today may be the beginning of your mighty comeback.

6. THE MOTHER AFTER MATERNITY LEAVE

You, the girl who reads this, not even the world's worst sinners feel guilty as heavy as a mother when she leaves her baby safe at home to go to work. Even if maternity leave lasted an eternity, a mother would still want one more day with her baby.

I understand the postpartum storm you suffer, the way it wrings a scream so loud inside your head that no one else can hear it. Your urge to quit is real, and so are the bills to be paid. You built an education and a careful career that you would drop in a heartbeat for your baby. If you cannot afford to pause, remember: providing is love. If you choose to stay home, that is love, too. Either way, you are choosing your child.

Even with milk painfully and uncomfortably expressed, pumped, and chilled, how do you give your all at an office desk when your heart is in the crib? With time, you will learn to hold two truths at once: worker and mother, provider, and nurturer.

When you return to work after that gap, it may look as if the world moved on too fast and too soon without you. Do not be dismayed. Even the most skilled artists and seasoned professionals take time to return to form after a break. You will, too, you will find your feet and thrive again.

So, breathe. This world was built by mothers who once doubted themselves. Stand on their shoulders; take strength from their stories. Childbirth is not a setback; it is a new strength. You may not feel it yet, but countless women found it after doing what felt impossible. They crossed this threshold. You will, too.

7. THE CHILDLESS WOMAN

You, the girl who reads this, working arms, strong legs, a sound mind, yet childless: it can feel like your own body has betrayed you. Then comes the pressure from family, questions at functions, careless remarks, social stigma, "kind" advice that cuts. Meanwhile, your days become a ledger of hope: appointments, blood tests, injections, pills, each scheduled, tracked, and second-guessed until you are exhausted.

And the worst part? Some mouths never stay shut. They did not stay shut when you were single. They did not stay shut when you got married. And they may not stay shut now. So, listen to me: protect your peace. Concentrate on your life. Refuse the noise of critics and fake well-wishers. To you, I say: if motherhood is what you truly want, keep moving with courage. And if the journey becomes different from what you imagined, remember this: motherhood is not only biology. There are many ways to become a mother. For every woman called "childless," there is also a child under the same sky who is "motherless." Love finds its way, sometimes from within, sometimes from outside.

8. THE WORKING WOMAN

You, the girl who reads this, a working mother, only a fighter like you can carry both family and work, and still manage to excel at both.

The world sees your commendable results. It rarely sees the sleepless nights and very early mornings, the meals you cooked for your family so you could still meet a deadline at work; the way you gave everyone your best and kept nothing for yourself.

You may not realize this, but many quietly envy the steadiness with which you balance home and work. That steadiness is not luck; it is hard work during midnights, alarms at dawns, and trade-offs that no one sees. Looking at you, I know this for sure: some of the best time managers in the world are working women. You keep going. Keep soaring. And when a small moment appears, take it for yourself. A few minutes of quiet is not "selfish", it's survival. So, keep doing what you do best, but relax whenever you can. You will succeed, at work, at home, and in the legacy your children will one day recognize with pride.

9. THE HOMEMAKER

You, the girl who reads this, a homemaker who works endlessly with little appreciation, this is the kind of exhaustion no one thinks to thank you for.

It took our country far too long to recognize housewives as homemakers. And if anyone ever asks you what a homemaker is, tell them this: a homemaker is a woman who sacrificed all her dreams so her families can come true. Like everyone, you had dreams once, too. And still, you gave so much of yourself, quietly, steadily, so the people you love could thrive.

One thing about homemakers is this: your loved ones often do not notice when you are unwell. How could they? Meals still appear. The home still runs. Food is ready before anyone even feels hungry, no matter what your body is carrying, no matter what your mind is enduring. They rarely notice your hunger, because everyone else is fed, vegetarian or non-vegetarian, fasting or not, because you make sure everyone is taken care of.

So, to you, I say: hold your head up, my dear. What you do matters. Even if it goes unnoticed and unspoken today, in the busyness of your family's life, your work is not small. Your love is not invisible.

Exhausted. Burned out. Demotivated. People act like these are "corporate" words, as if only offices earn the right to say them. But they belong to you, too, even if they are not in your dictionary. Yes, given the chance, you will do it all over again for your family. But that does not cancel your need for rest.

Keep going, but also remember: you deserve care too. Rest when you can. Ask for help when you must. You are not a machine. You are the heart of a home.

10. THE SINGLE WORKING WOMAN

You, the girl who reads this, a single working woman, people will have opinions. Relatives will comment. Colleagues will judge. Some friends may call it concern, but quietly measure you against their expectations. Even parents may pressure you. Let them.

You are an adult. You are learned. You know what to do. Maybe you have everything planned out already. Maybe you are still figuring it out. Maybe you will choose to settle down someday, when you want to. Either way, freedom is your birthright. Use it wisely.

Keep your boundaries firm, and keep your eyes on your path. The world may pity you because you are not living by the rules it wrote for you. Let it. You are living by your dreams, and building a life you chose.

To you, I say: keep soaring. Let your success and happiness serve as proof to every young woman still searching for her courage and independence. We are where we are because women before you fought for the right to work, to earn an honest living, and to carry heavy burdens so they could support themselves, rather than be funded by family and told what to do. So, keep doing good, and keep walking forward, so the young women who follow you won't have to fight as hard as you did.

11. THE SPORTSWOMAN

You, the girl who reads this, hearing discouraging words, receiving less attention than men's sports, and fighting for resources can drain the spirit.

It is normal for any girl to want soft skin, to smell good with perfume, to have tender hands and that traditional feminine look. But you chose something else.

You chose the sun. The heat. The burn. The kind of tan that does not fade quickly. You chose bruises that bloom, fade, and come back again. You chose scars that do not ask permission to stay. You chose hands that harden, because you are building a body built for your game, not a body made only to be "feminine."

Let the sweat stay. Let it smell. It is the scent of work. The scent of learning. The scent of showing up again and again, until comfort becomes irrelevant and skill becomes undeniable.

So many sacrifices for your game, so much of you poured into it.

And that is exactly why you matter. That is why your effort matters.

Our country needs more sportswomen like you, women who keep training even when the spotlight is elsewhere. You are doing your best to excel, and that dedication counts, even when no one claps. Some people play for fame. Some play for money. Most people play for fun. But very few play for the pure spirit of the game, and you are one of them.

So, to you, I say: do not give up. Seen or unseen, funded or not, keep going. Some men may need sports, but sports need women. You are not "trying." You are becoming. And champion is not only a title, it is an identity.

12. THE SOON-TO-BE DIVORCED

You, the girl who reads this, whatever the reason, mutual or contested, no divorce is easy. The anticipatory anxiety, the social pressure, and the long process can keep anyone awake at night. It can be exhausting to imagine the paperwork, the conversations, the arguments within the family, the future judgment, and the waiting. Some days you will feel brave; other days you will feel numb. One day you will feel certain, and the next day you will question yourself, because even when it is necessary, endings such as these are never clean.

People will have opinions you never asked for. Some will blame you. Some will pity you. Some will advise you as if they lived your life. Let them talk.

They did not carry your marriage on their shoulders, in your mind, in your body, in your silent prayers. They did not hear what you heard behind closed doors. They do not know the nights you cried quietly, the mornings you forced a smile, the times you tried "one last time" just to keep the peace.

They were not the one who walked into family functions and gatherings wearing a brave face, or the one who avoided them just to save themselves from shame. They only saw what you allowed them to see.

Only you know. And you do not owe anyone an explanation

So, to you, I say: hang in there. If you survived a painful marriage long enough to reach this decision, you can certainly survive the final stretch to end it. You have endured so much already. And you are not "starting over," you are starting again, with wisdom. Gather your strength. The fight ahead is worth your freedom.

13. THE DIVORCED WOMAN

You, the girl who reads this, divorce is not only a legal ending. It is an emotional earthquake. As if separation is not painful enough, divorce can shrink people you once called "family" into just familiar faces. You may feel fear, anger, shame, and self-pity, sometimes all at once. You may walk into gatherings and feel exposed, as if every glance contains a question, a judgment, or unsolicited advice.

I wish the world understood what you are carrying: the anxiety of what people will say, and the heavier anxiety of what they will not say, the silence, the stares, the assumptions.

So, to you, I say: be gentle with yourself, and be vigilant too. Vulnerable seasons attract both help and exploitation, and sometimes they look similar at first. It is okay if you misread a person once or twice. Learn, adjust, continue.

And yes, be patient with all your might, because this season will test you. Paperwork will test you. Family will test you. Memories will test you. Even your own mind will test you. But patience does not mean swallowing everything; it means choosing your next step without letting chaos choose it for you.

Remember this: the end of one chapter is not the end of life. There are pages ahead with more peace, more joy, and more strength than you can imagine right now, not because the past was "meant" to happen, but because you are still here, still capable, still writing. Stay patient. Stay steady. You are still writing your story.

14. THE DIVORCED MOTHER

You, the girl who reads this, as heavy as divorce is, it often weighs heaviest on a divorced mother. Because along with grief comes loneliness, and along with loneliness comes responsibility: raising your child with two hands doing the work of four. I understand the pressure of doing it alone in a world that has not always been kind to you.

I wish the world understood this: the stigma placed on a divorced mother is already a heavy load, and your innocent child should never be made to carry it too. People will ask. People will assume. But their words are nothing compared to the moment your child asks, softly, why.

Strangers can be dismissed. A child cannot. Your child may be too young to understand what changed, too innocent to hold the reasons, yet old enough to ask questions that make you ache in places you did not know existed.

No matter how broken a mother feels, the effort she pours out with whatever spirit she has left is never wasted, it becomes part of her child's future. Even if you feel weak some days, the way you nurture, protect, educate, and prepare your child for life, even with a broken spirit, is powerful. You still show up. You still build a life for your child. We need a word stronger than "strong" for your efforts. The sacrifices you make in silence, the times you swallow your tears and still show up, matter more than anyone can measure right now.

So, to you, I say this: there is no force in this world stronger than a mother who keeps loving through pain. Keep going, one day, one breath, one small step at a time. Keep choosing steadiness. Keep choosing love. What you are building for your child, will outlast what tried to break you.

15. THE WIDOWED MOTHER

You, the girl who reads this, a widowed mother who has devoted her life to nurturing and supporting her child, your resilience is immeasurable. Oh, what responsibilities have fallen on your already heavy shoulders! As if the role of a mother was not heavy enough now you have to undertake the role of a father too. You must be comfort and discipline, softness and firmness, provider, and protector, two roles folded into one tired body and spirit. It is understandable to wish it were all a bad dream, that you would wake up and find your husband beside you, and life returned to what it used to be. If only reality were that kind.

When a bond meant to last a lifetime breaks, grief can do unspeakable things to the mortal heart. And yet you show up, again and again, for your child: for its future, for its safety, for the gentle childhood every child deserves. That is devotion.

Know that you are not alone. A widowed mother with children may feel lonely, but she is never without love, and never without a life that still needs her. Even in quiet rooms, even in long nights, even when your child tests you with its naughtiness and sometimes its rudeness, your love is all around you, in the life you are keeping safe. And if you feel unseen, let this be seen: what you are doing is extraordinary. Not because you never fall apart, but because you keep returning. Because you keep loving.

With your permission, may I say this? If, someday, the thought of companionship returns to you, quietly, unexpectedly, please do not punish yourself for it. It does not mean you have forgotten. It does not mean your love was smaller. It only means you are human, and you are still alive.

You may worry about what your family will say or what your child will think. But know that your happiness matters too. If your heart is ready, do not be ashamed of choosing life again. Your love and your loyalty have already been proven by how you survived. Take the leap when you are ready. You deserve tenderness too - in whatever form it comes.

16. THE MOURNING WOMAN

You, the girl who reads this, grieving someone you love, what you are feeling is heartbreak in its purest form. Some people have easy distractions. Some have noise, crowds, and ways to numb what they feel. But you may not. You may be indoors, alone with your thoughts, carrying the full weight of your sorrow, and that takes strength.

To sit in loneliness, fighting your own mind and learning to live with grief alone, is not weakness. It is courage. So, to you, I say: cry if that is what your heart needs. There is nothing weak about tears.

Gifts, hugs, and kisses are for the living. For our departed loved ones, only tears remain, the tribute we offer in remembrance. Tears, water, a little salt, and a world of emotion, are simple, honest proof that your love was real. So, cry, my dear girl. If tears are going to flow, let them flow like a river. Let all the sadness come and let it go when it is ready.

And when you can, take one small step at a time. Start with what your body needs: drink water, eat something and get some fresh air. If you can, talk to someone.

Grief does not demand heroism. It only asks that you keep going, moment by moment. I will not lie to you and say time "heals" everything. But with time, it may hurt a little differently. The love will still be there, and slowly, you will learn how to live around the ache.

17. THE ACCIDENTAL HERO

You, the girl who reads this, if a hero is someone who rescues the helpless in the hour of need, then tell me: are you not a hero too?

Since when did heroism become reserved for only a few grand acts? No role is too small. If you have ever stepped into a role that wasn't meant for you, because no one else stepped in, and sometimes no one else was even there, then you, the girl who reads this, are a hero too.

Not the kind from stories, the kind who becomes a mother without giving birth, a parent to siblings, a guardian to a child, a caretaker to aging parents, a mentor to someone who had no guide, a friend to the friendless. Even if it was not forever, even if it was just one season, one moment, one rescue, you still stepped in.

Some responsibilities find you without warning. Someone innocent and defenseless reaches for help. The world replies, not my problem, not my responsibility. And you, without announcing it, without making it dramatic, refused to let them fall. You held on. You offered your hand. You helped them rise.

For someone who was in the wrong place at the wrong time, you became the right person at the right time. And that makes you an accidental hero.

Unfortunate things happen quietly, and quiet heroism is easy to misunderstand. Sometimes even you can question yourself. You can wonder if you took on too much, if you made the wrong decision by choosing too much responsibility. But understand the truth: when everyone else gave their zero, you gave your hundred. No one else could have carried it the way you did, not with that steadiness, not with that patience, not with that kind of love.

A common trait among good people is this: you feel too guilty to call responsibility a burden, and too pressured to experience love with peace. You might feel like you cannot afford mistakes, not when someone else is depending on you heavily. And to anyone who went out of their way to help someone in need, if you know you did the right thing, but it was still too much for you: relax. You are only human.

It is enough that you keep showing up, even tired, even stretched, even silent.

And when responsibility pulls you day after day, do not forget what you've done. Don't forget the personal records you broke, the milestones you crossed, the quiet sacrifices you made. Do not forget the future you planted like a seed, not for yourself, but for someone else. A seed that will live long after you, and speak your name long after you are gone.

So let this chapter remind you, clearly: you did not take too much, you became what was missing in another person's life.

And even if nobody thanked you the way you deserved, even if it cost you more than people will ever know, this much is true:

What was an accident in your life became the greatest blessing in the life you are taking care of.

18. THE OLD WOMAN

You, the girl who reads this, glasses on, tired eyes, an aching body. You carry so many stories, so many lessons, yet the world rarely slows down to listen. There was a time when people waited for your decisions. Now they may not even ask your opinion. Humans are generous with flowers at funerals, but stingy with love while people are still breathing.

If there is one thing, we haven't learned yet, it's how to cherish people in the present, before time turns them into memories. You might wish for more respect, more love and a little of your loved ones' time, but you also know the old truth: people miss the sun only after dusk.

In your world, many are forgiven, even those who disrespect you. Ripened by age, you carry a heart with no ego and zero grudges. Your eyes have witnessed many births, and, sadly, many departures. Your body may beg for rest, while your heart still clings to the faces you love.

So, to you, I say: live a little longer. Live to see your family take one more step forward. And when your soul is finally ready, may you receive the rest you deserve. Until then, live.

19. THE TRANSWOMAN

You, the girl who reads this, finally, when the whole book is dedicated to women, did you think we might forget you? If only the world could understand the medical process that was both emotionally and physically draining for you to transition, it would accept you as a woman and stop denying the respect you deserve.

In a world where the two genders debate who has it the hardest, came the third gender, who courageously embraced womanhood, aware of its pain. How strong you must be when God and nature themselves gave you the wrong body, you decided to rewrite your own story and set things right.

So, hear this: do not let society's cruelty mold you into a stereotype. Hold on to your kindness without surrendering your boundaries. Truth be told, equality for transgender people is a necessary revolution that is most overdue. Until we reach there, dare to be good, kind, and respectful even to a world that seldom offered these virtues to you. And to young trans women: study, my dear. Build your career. Rise high, so you can protect yourself, support others, and help the world be kind and respectful to you and to other trans women who follow.

20. TO YOU, THE GIRL WHO READS THIS

You, the girl who reads this, it is hard to fit you into categories, because you were never meant to be contained. So, it is only natural that you may not find all your struggles, your achievements, or your victories fully written in these limited pages. No pen carries enough ink, and no book carries enough space, to hold everything you have endured, the pain, the challenges, the sacrifices, the humiliations, the storms you crossed, and the way you still stood up to do it all over again.

You have lived many lives inside one life.

You have been a sister and a friend. A teacher and a guide. A healer while tending to your own wounds. You have been the calm voice in chaos, the steady hands in crisis, the one who remembers, the one who holds, the one who keeps going when everyone else rests. You have been a mother in the fullest sense of the word. And when life demanded more, you became more. You became shelter and strength, for a child who misses a father and still needs a home.

And through all of it, you did not lose your humanity.

You are beautiful, not because the world approves, but because you carry the truth. You are different, unique, and irreplaceable. You are strong, kind, humble, courageous, selfless, bold, and relentless. You bring value to this world not only by what you do, but by who you are, by the love you give, the resilience you embody, and the light you protect even on your darkest days.

If no one has told you lately, let this letter do it properly:

You matter.

You have always mattered.

And you will continue to matter, long after this page, long after this book, long after the ending.

I wish you Godspeed!

THE STORIES OF THE WOMEN WHO MADE THIS BOOK POSSIBLE

There's history to celebrate winners and achievers. Let the present champion the dreamers and fighters.

1 THE GOOD SISTER

She jokingly said, "For anyone who doesn't believe in inequality, they ought to visit a middle-class Indian house to see how they treat the brother and the sister." As her brother's elder sister, she loved him deeply, but the amount of freedom he was gifted with was enormous compared to hers. There was a curfew for their daughter, while his brother could come and go home at any time. He could play all day long with his friends while she had to help her mother cook food in the kitchen. She thought this would change with age, but her curfew remained the same from school to college, college to university, and university to office.

Whoever puts in more effort gets more results, and that is what happened to her, too. They both studied at the same school, but her marks were higher than his. Two years older and two grades higher than her brother in school, her marks were a record he could never break. Not that he could not, but he didn't because he was far more interested in cricket, cinemas and online mobile games with his friends. Growing up together, their parents did not even know where their son was, but when their daughter asked to go out with her friends, it was often a hard "no". A "yes" was rare and often came with many questions. Questions like who she is going out with, where they're going, and when she'll come back. Even going on college tours with her professors and classmates required a lot of convincing. She had countless arguments about this bias in their house, and every time, the answer was the same, but in different forms: "it's all for your own good," "the world is a bad place," and "we can't bear it if something happens to you." As she grew older and after countless failed attempts, she realized it was a lost cause, and the girl stopped asking her parents for anything. Nevertheless, they were her parents, so she helped them however she could while she was still living with them. From cooking to cleaning, she helped both her mother and father. Even though she had to stay indoors most of the time, she made the most of it, reading widely alongside her schoolwork, learning skills like sewing and cooking, and consistently ranking at the top of her class.

As the years passed, academic life came to an end, and professional life began. Everyone thought that the sister would outshine her brother, but sadly, that was not the case. Their adult lives were not the same as their student lives. While she worked in the same small hometown where she was born, her brother worked in three cities during his career before moving to France. He earns well and visits India once a year. She, on the other hand, is now married and has a daughter of her own; she still works in the same hometown and stays near her parents' house so she can be near them.

There is a saying, "comfort zone is a beautiful place, but nothing ever grows there." That is what happened in her case too. Being forced to play it safe over the years, lacking sufficient outside knowledge, led her to restrict herself to careers within her hometown. Her brother, on the other hand, knew people, had friends outside his small hometown because of how he grew up, was not afraid to take risks, travel, or be away from friends and family, and that is why he is more successful than her.

Her story–in her voice

"Although my parents always compared my brother's marks with mine and tried to motivate him to score more. I never saw my brother as a competition. When I was growing up, I studied hard and got good marks, and for my age, as an elder sister, I saw my brother struggle with his academics. I wanted to be successful in my career so I could help him get a job. So, I am happy that he succeeded on his own.

When I was young, because of all the restrictions I had, I always thought my parents loved me less, and that's why they wouldn't give me the same freedom they gave my brother, but that all changed when I saw my parents, who didn't cry at my brother's wedding, cry for mine.

So, I know my parents love me the most. However, the way I was brought up has altered the way I live. Growing up, I did not even enjoy going out, I was, and still am, an introvert. I just hated that my brother was allowed to, and I was not. It made me feel controlled, and it made me want to go out even more. My parents bought the bike that my brother asked for, but my only means of transport was the bus. My brother fell off his bike many times while learning to drive, but I was too precious, and, according to my parents, there were a lot of idiots on the road, so I was not allowed to drive. I want to drive a bike now, but I'm a mother of a toddler, and I can't afford to fall and get hurt since I have to take care of her. I'm also afraid of driving now. When the age was right for me to get hurt and be adventurous, my parents suppressed it. I want to grow now, but life with all its commitments will not let me do it.

I am not blaming my parents. I have a daughter of my own now, so I have the same fears as a parent now that my parents had when they had me. But I will not restrict my daughter in the same way. Of course, it can be a dangerous world, but not if we are smart enough, and that's exactly how I will raise my daughter. To be smart in a dangerous world. At the same time, I will not force my failures on my daughter. She will have her own life, and I'll fix mine. I understand I can't be as successful as my brother, but I will be successful in my own career, not for me to fix my life, but so I can provide a better life for my daughter and that I can take care of my aging parents. They love me so much, and they're so possessive of me, and they need me now more than ever. Oh, and how can I forget, I'm an elder sister, I want to treat my brother well every time he visits us in India. But if I could leave one message for any sister who currently lives her life the way I did, it would be this: do not carry your childhood cage into your adulthood. A bird that has been caged for far too long forgets what freedom feels like, even after the door is open. Do not live like that.

Take calculated risks. Explore. Make mistakes. Learn. Grow.

And remember: the hard work you poured into your education will pay off. Just do not stop at graduation, your future will also be shaped by the decisions you make after.

2 THE FRIEND WHO TEACHES

One month into her new job, she ordered coffee at her office canteen during her break. She was thankful to have got the government job she always wanted. Sipping the nice hot coffee and listening to the noise of people in the canteen talking, birds chirping, and leaves on trees dancing, she recalled the jobless days not so long ago. When she did not have a job of her own after graduating, she watched all her friends find good jobs - some even went abroad, some even married rich, and some joined their family business. On the other hand, the so-called gifted child, unlike her friends, did not have any of their luxuries. Even after numerous attempts she did not find a job for a long time. When success is long overdue in your own life, even the good at heart start envying their friends' success rather than wishing them the best. During those tough days, she recalled helping her friends with their studies. The boys and girls in her class assembled at her house for group study. She explained the most complex points using stories, so her friends could remember them point by point and write down the information during the exam. A walking library and the unofficial teacher were her nicknames in both school and university. Even when it was just 10 minutes before the exam started, when she wanted to study one more answer to score extra marks, her below-average friends would ask her to explain concepts. She never apologized, saying she had no time to teach at the last minute, but she always helped them, sacrificing her own high marks to help her friends barely pass the subject. Thanks to her, all her friends graduated and got good jobs. She attended housewarming parties and weddings of her friends, where they would introduce her to everyone as the girl behind their success. But she silently suffered because, as the person responsible for everyone else's success, hers was still due. She tried taking on some low-paying jobs, but she was not satisfied, so she decided to quit, took her time, and studied hard again. Only this time, there was no one else to ask for help with studies. With peace and solitude, she studied for two years and cracked the competitive exam, comfortably securing the government job she had aspired to.

If she had only been a little bit selfish and kept her knowledge to herself instead of helping a few classmates, she would be in a much better position now. Success would have come to her a little early too. But when asked about this, all she said was, "Knowledge and education are not meant to be hoarded; they are meant to be shared."

3 THE BRIDE-TO-BE

My parents had three girls; I am the youngest, followed by my two older sisters. As in many families, my eldest sister is the most responsible of the three of us. My middle sister serves as a mediator between our parents and me whenever we have a quarrel. And then there's me, the last-born, pampered as the youngest usually is. People often say they lacked this or that in childhood. I do not remember a single thing I wished for and didn't get. My eldest sister is seven years older than I, and my middle sister is four years older. If my parents could not get me something, my eldest sister did. If she could not, my middle sister shared what she had. Life was kind to me. I mostly got everything I needed, and sometimes I even got the things I did not even know I wanted, thanks to the care and affection of my dad, my mom, and my two sisters.

We were not well off back then. My father did not earn much from his business at first. Because of that, my eldest sister could not study the exact course she wanted or attend her first-choice university. By the time it was my middle sister's turn, Dad had begun to make some progress; she did not get her first-choice course or university either, but she managed to get her second choice. When it came to me, I was not the strongest student, but by then Dad's business was doing well, and I got to pick the course and university I wanted. As I said, there is not a thing in life I wanted that I didn't get. My parents and sisters each faced their own struggles to reach where they are today; for me, so much was served to me on a golden plate.

I do not know what it feels like to be shouted at. I do not know the ache of wanting something and being denied. They say, "Your comfort zone is a beautiful place, but nothing grows there." I have lived most of my life in a comfort zone. But everything changes one day, doesn't it? Anyone listening so far would think: she has everything. Yes, I do, for now. But what happens when I marry and go to another house? Will I still have everything? Will things still come easily?

I am not selfish. I do not expect life to be easy in my future husband's home. I am willing to learn. I am willing to compromise and adjust in certain things. I can wake up early or stay up late some days to finish the chores. But I have heard stories from friends about how they were treated in their husbands' houses, especially by mothers-in-law. I have never been shouted at. I have never been ordered around. What if that changes after marriage? My wedding is in three months, and I am sweating just thinking about it. Should marriage be this scary?

During nervous spells like these, I recall a late-night conversation with a friend. I am a bride-to-be, and just like me, I know many other brides feel the same fear before they start their new chapters. So, I'm sharing the speech my friend gave me, with every nervous bride in mind. I hope it steadies you the way it steadies me. "Why worry so much about bad things that might not even happen? When you finished school and went to college, you told yourself you would never get your school days back, and then you loved college. When you finished college and started working, you said you would never get your college days back, and yet work brought its own joys. Now you are working and about to marry, and you're saying you won't get your bachelor life back. No one gets any part of life back. You enjoyed school, college, and work. In college, you depended on your parents for money; now you can buy what you want. You say you are "free" now, but do your parents let you take trips out of the city whenever you like? If you are late after 6 p.m., how many missed calls do you get from your father? How many dream destinations have you crossed off your list? You do not know it yet, but you will do those things with your husband after you marry.

All new things are scary at first. Do not be so easily scared. I have watched you since school: apart from studying hard and writing your own lab records, you've even written the lab records for the boys in our class. You helped some of our weakest friends pass exams. You came from a Tamil-medium school and still delivered the longest presentations in English at your university. At work, you have met tight deadlines and handled difficult managers, toxic colleagues, and demanding clients. The only thing you knew how to cook back then was hot water, but now, you can cook pretty much any dish you can think of. No one taught you these things. You have come far, and you have gathered so many skills. Do you think you cannot handle marriage? Do you think the good values your parents taught you and the lessons you learned will not help you as a wife? Here is what will happen: you'll use that experience to choose a good partner and build a good life. I am not saying it will be perfect, nothing is. Not with parents, colleagues, clients, or neighbors. There will be conflicts, and you will work through them. Even if life is not happy, you'll try to make it happy. Trust yourself. Sometimes you will change him; other times you'll change yourself. And do not think marriage means leaving your parents completely. You have been "leaving" them in small ways since you were three, when you started school. You left a little more when you stayed late in college or did sleepovers at friends' houses. You left even more when you started working. Did they leave you? They will not. A parent's love is more powerful than the distance marriage creates. So, do not doubt their love for you.

I am not a fortune-teller, but I know you, and based on that, I believe you'll make it work. There are so many women who have carried their battles alone, and sometimes they do not realize how much they have already achieved. When doubt rises, first calm yourself. Then reflect on what you have faced and what you have overcome. Do just this, for now: focus completely on the struggles you met, and how you moved through each one. You are thinking of marriage as a new struggle, but every struggle you conquered was once new, too. When you look only at what you have managed, solved, and survived so far, you'll know you can work the rest out as well. For all you know, a better life than this is waiting, while you are busy fearing it."

Recalling my friend's speech, I believe in myself, and my hands stop shaking. I hope it stills yours, too.

4 THE NEW MOTHER

There are two special days in my life: the day I got my first period and the day I became a mother. Both brought pain. The first pain made me a woman; the second made me a mother.

I have a PhD in Human Resources. I earned my doctorate, and I earned my motherhood, too. Pregnancy was not easy. Like many women, I struggled to keep food down; I vomited whenever I ate, could not sleep well, and kept getting cramps in many parts of my body. Sleeplessness and pain - I could manage that, but my real fear was that every time I threw up, the baby was not getting enough food for itself. Each hospital visit was nerve-racking. I prayed only to hear the doctor say, "Baby is healthy." I was ready to take whatever and however many pills that were prescribed to me just so I could give birth to my baby in a perfectly healthy condition.

Finally, the moment we were waiting for came - I was in the hospital waiting for 2 days for the actual labor to start, and after a painful labor, I welcomed my first baby to the world. For women like me, those first tears of joy fall the moment we first see our baby. That day, when the nurse handed me that delicate, tiny, weightless thing, my life changed forever. In my house, I am not alone. My grandmother, mother, father, and husband all help care for my baby. Even so, with so many people to take care of my baby, I never sleep peacefully. When my child cries, something in me switches on. There is an unexplainable feeling that puts me in panic mode and shouts to me that my baby is my responsibility. Of course, my family was with me during pregnancy, but I am the only one who carried her for ten months with me, how can I be calm when my baby cries? Even my baby's simple cries sound like the gravest danger to me.

I broke my right leg and left hand badly when I was four years old. I am thirty now, and I still limp and can't lift heavy things. I live with that pain. Pain is not new to me, but the pain I went through during childbirth - I've never felt anything like that before and that pain changed me. I had a normal delivery. I pushed a baby out of my body, and for days it felt as if I had torn myself open. Even now, I do not sleep the same. My energy is different, my appetite is different; even my mental sharpness feels altered.

I used to love education, and I still love education. Wherever learning happens, I want to be there. With its beautiful campus, learned faculty and large libraries, I love my university and dream of a full-time position there, but I also want to be present for my baby. My parents educated me well not only by enrolling me in school, but also through extracurricular activities such as tailoring, typewriting, shorthand, languages, and sports. I want to use the education my parents gave me, to teach, to pass on what I have learned to the next generation, but, subconsciously, I keep telling myself that my child needs me, too. It feels like I am forced to live two separate lives, but sadly, I have only one body to be in one place at a time. I think many mothers feel this: educated, competent, and yet childbirth can feel like a setback. Even thinking like this makes me feel guilty, but this is what goes on in my mind. It is like - I want to do this and that, but I can only do this or that. I had my baby through a normal vaginal birth, and recovery was hard for me. If recovery was hard for me, my heart goes out to mothers who have had C-sections and faced their own scars and strength.

As a PhD, I have trained 500+ students, delivered more than 100 seminars, published research papers, and won a few awards. Along the way, I have met many women achievers, and many who were on the verge of becoming so. I know my background; I know my drive. I am trying to stay relevant and up to date, but some days it feels impossible to mother my child and do everything else at the same time. My daughter is not even one yet. Part of me thinks I should take a three-year break, at least until she starts school, and then resume my career. But I have done enough research to know how this story often goes: responsibilities do not end when a child starts school; they only change shape. Waking them up. Getting them ready. (Do you know how hard it is to wake a child on time?)

People joke that women take a long time to get ready. Some men are late, too. But if an adult is getting ready, it is in their own hands; getting a child ready is not. Children being children, they do not always cooperate. There is so much responsibility that falls on a parent's shoulders here. Most mothers wake up at 5 a.m. to cook for the school tiffin. While the child is at school, every mother prays she will not get that emergency call, fever, a fall, something wrong. And when the child returns from school, there is no rest: laundry, cooking, watching tiny hands and feet so they do not hurt themselves. Just thinking about it makes my head spin. I am a new mother; I haven't lived all of this yet, but I've listened, I've read stories, and I know my turn will soon come. And waking at 5 a.m. is a luxury if the school is nearby; some families live far away, or in cities where traffic hardly moves, they rise at three or four.

And then there's work. If a mother wakes at 5, does the housework, sends a child to school, and goes to the office, how steady will her mood be? How sharp can her mind stay? It is a quiet, daily battle not to let mood swings bruise others, not to make hasty decisions out of emotion, not to let sleeplessness cause mistakes. Everyone wants competence. New mothers once were the competent ones. A little support could help them find that self again, but too many workplaces will not give them the time or the opportunity to give them a chance.

I am not asking for pity. I am asking for understanding, and for space wide enough to hold both truths: I am a scholar, and I am a mother. I have done hard things before. I worked hard for 4 years to earn my PhD so I can add a "Dr." in front of my name, and I worked hard for 10 months to earn my "mother" title. Both give me pride equally. I have done hard and harder things before. I can do them again. I have worked hard before, and now I am going to learn to work hard for my baby.

5 THE NEWLYWED

The night was warm, silent, and dark, but inside the house, voices crashed over her from every side. No one softened. No one stepped in. Days without sleep had scraped her raw; her body shook with exhaustion, her mind breaking under the pressure.

Then her eyes caught the knife.

She grabbed it before she could think, before she could remember her son who had been sleeping beside her only minutes ago.

Slash, slash, slash, slash…

Thirteen quick cuts across her left arm in the blink of an eye, an attempt to silence the storm.

Blood dripped onto the kitchen floor. Her husband stood there. Her sister-in-law watched. The sharp smell of blood filled the small kitchen and didn't leave.

This should have been the moment of panic, someone rushing forward, someone asking why. Instead, the house stayed eerily quiet.

"Why is she behaving like a psycho?" the sister-in-law said, coldly.

She was surrounded, husband, mother-in-law, father-in-law, sister-in-law. Four people in one room, and still nobody asked the simplest question: Why? No one held her. No one tried to calm her.

Only when her body swayed, and she started to faint did her husband finally move. He took her to the hospital.

On the way, he called her family, not out of fear for her, but to make sure the responsibility did not fall on him.

Her father rushed in that night, sweating through his T-shirt, panicked beyond words. "What happened to her? How did it happen?" he demanded, fear sharp in his voice.

The son-in-law said nothing.

One look at his daughter's arm, and the father understood. Anger rose, then broke into grief. "Why did you do this to yourself?" he demanded, but love softened the scream. The old man started crying in the hospital like a child.

And the daughter, she could not speak. She only cried.

Self-inflicted wounds. A mother. A child who depended on her.

What pushed her to that edge?

To understand, you must go back, not to one night, but to everything that led her there.

Her childhood

She was the second child in her family, born at a time when many still preferred boys. But her father did not. He had wanted a girl.

When he heard she was born, he was at sea, working on a ship. In delight, he begged the captain to turn back and take the whole ship home. The captain laughed, but understood the urgency of a new father and arranged a smaller boat that could take him to shore sooner.

Her father rushed to the hospital and saw her: a chubby, dark-skinned baby girl, tiny, perfect, with faint hair on her legs, just like his mother had. He was proud. He loved her fiercely from the first moment. In his heart, he believed his departed mother had returned to him through her. Such was the love she received after she was born. Even when she was grown, studying at university, whenever she walked down the road with her father and some men so much as glanced at her, he did the same thing every time. He placed a hand on her shoulder, lifted his aviator sunglasses just enough for his eyes to show, and gave them a look with an attitude that said, "This is my little girl." That look made every single one of them look away.

That was the kind of love she grew up with, fierce, protective, almost possessive.

She grew up with education and comfort. She was protected, loved, and given opportunities. She was also unusually gentle, the kind of person who prayed even for people who treated her badly. She wasn't weak. She was simply soft-hearted. Even as an adult, she struggled with confrontation. Always got interrupted when she was speaking but she didn't learn how to interrupt when others were speaking. She didn't know how to argue in a room full of voices. She grew up innocent, so innocent that even as an adult, if she went somewhere unfamiliar, she sometimes did not know how to find her way back home, even in the very city she had grown up in. Strangers would sometimes assume she was new to the city and gently guide her to the right bus.

She finished school, college, and took a job. She did not have to work, her family was doing well, but she wanted to support herself. She did not want a loud life. She wanted a peaceful one.

Marriage did not frighten her the way it frightened many women around her. She trusted her parents to find her the right person.

They did.

On paper.

He was a professional. He had stability. He had his own house. His parents were retired. His sister lived in America. The alliance looked perfect. After college, she learned to cook seriously, took lessons from her mother, wrote down recipes, because she wanted to give her best to her future husband.

Before the wedding, she stopped working because she planned to relocate after the marriage. She said goodbye to friends and neighbors she'd known since childhood. Then she left her parents and entered her husband's house as a bride.

Her family sent her off with tears and love, the way Indian homes often do. Her father cried the hardest. Proud that she was starting her new life, and in pain that his baby was leaving his roof.

She told herself she was ready. She had dreamed of a fairytale marriage, of love, of warmth, of becoming close to her in-laws through care and respect.

The first month

In the beginning, she tried hard. She woke early, not out of fear of what people might think of her in the new house, but out of love. She learned quickly that her husband loved food, so she cooked before he woke up and made sure everything was ready, hot, and fresh.

Then the mood in the house began to shift. It shifted through small changes: more vessels to wash, more sweeping, more cooking, more tasks handed to her as if she had endless energy and no needs of her own. She did everything without complaint because she believed adjustment was part of being a good wife.

Sometimes she wanted to tell her husband how she felt, not to create drama, but to be heard. But she stopped herself. She feared that if she spoke, he would fight his parents for her, and she didn't want to be blamed as the "new girl" who broke a family.

So, she stayed quiet.

That quietness became a habit.

Over time, she noticed something that hurt: her in-laws behaved one way when their son was home and another way when he was away for work. When he was away, the workload increased and the tone became sharper. She had already left her parents, her home, her friends, her job, everything familiar. The loneliness was heavy. The disrespect made it heavier.

The sister-in-law visits

The first visit from the U.S. sister-in-law changed the already bad atmosphere quickly. The family treated her visit like a festival, special meals, special attention, and the new bride was expected to handle most of it. She did not mind at first. She told herself, she is family too.

But the visit brought something else: jokes that were not really jokes. Smiles that carried humiliation. Comments about her being unemployed, "local," "just a house girl." At first it was disguised. Then it became direct.

She smiled through it, especially in front of her husband, because she did not want him to feel uncomfortable. She acted like it did not touch her. But inside, she was being worn down, day by day.

So, she asked her husband if she could resume her career. She thought earning would stop the insults and restore her dignity.

He refused.

He told his parents. They refused too.

They said they had enough money and that it would be "insulting" for the daughter-in-law to go out and work. Their own daughter working in America wasn't seen as insulting, but the same rules did not apply to her.

The contradiction suffocated her: mocked for not earning, blocked from earning.

Eventually, she told her husband everything, the insults, the workload, the way she was treated when he was not present. He listened and asked, "What do you want me to do?"

She asked for one thing: a separate house nearby. Close enough to visit his parents anytime, but separate enough for peace.

In a traditional household, this request came across as an accusation. The in-laws heard it as a sign of separation, disrespect, or betrayal. Arguments spread. She was blamed for wanting to "take their son away." She was sent back to her parents' home.

Days passed, and no one came to take her back.

Her father, loving and desperate, went to their house and apologized publicly, so she could return. Watching her father bow down for her request stayed in her heart like a scar of its own.

After that, things calmed only because the sister-in-law went back to the U.S. The "storm" didn't end, but it paused.

Pregnancy and after

She still loved her husband. She believed he was a good man, kind at heart, but easily influenced. And when she became pregnant, for a brief time, she thought things might finally soften.

During those months, her husband began caring for her more. He saw her body changing, her strength stretched thin, her sleep broken, her breath heavier. He began to respect what it means to carry a child, how a woman's body becomes a home before the baby ever sees a home.

But his parents watched that care with suspicion, not tenderness. They treated his love as weakness. They filled his ears with poison disguised as advice: If you take care of her too much, she will get used to it. If you treat her gently, she will start controlling you. If you stand by her now, she will believe she owns this house.

Because in their eyes, the girl who came from another house and married their son should be a wife, but their son should remain their son, not her husband.

She saw the pattern clearly. One moment he would be warm and protective; the next day, after a single conversation with them, he would become distant, as if caring for his pregnant wife was something he had to apologize for.

Then she gave birth to a baby boy.

The family celebrated the baby. They held him, cared for him, loved him. And she watched it all while recovering almost alone. In a house full of people, she still felt like she did not exist.

Even when her husband tried to help her, bring water, check on her pain, sit beside her, the disapproval in his parents' eyes was enough to stop him. Their stares controlled him. Their silence controlled him. And she paid the price.

She had carried a whole baby, pushed him into the world through her own body, and when she could barely care for herself, when she needed her life partner the most, he stepped back, listening to his parents instead of standing by her.

There is a special kind of cruelty in that: to treat a woman as invisible at the exact moment her body has been through the most. To let her ache and bleed quietly, while everyone gathers around the baby and forgets the mother who brought it into the world.

The loneliness she felt then didn't leave quickly. It settled inside her like a cold weight.

Still, she held herself together for her child. She didn't collapse because she couldn't afford to. Her son became her anchor, her reason to keep waking up, to keep cooking, to keep enduring. Years passed. He grew, went to school, and loved his mother deeply. Life became routine endurance, difficult, but manageable.

Then the U.S. sister-in-law visited again, this time with her own child. It did not just bring extra work. It brought comparison. Her son began being treated like "less." At first, she tried to ignore it, telling herself it was temporary. But then came the scolding, the harshness aimed at her child for simply being a child. The criticism increased, and she could not stay silent anymore.

One day she raised her voice.

Her husband, who should have stood up for his son, did not.

That broke something in her.

Her in-laws turned on her fully: four voices against one. They blamed her for her son's behavior. They accused her of "poisoning" the grandson against them. They scolded her in front of her crying child.

She tried to explain, but she didn't know the art of interrupting. She waited for them to stop speaking. They did not stop. If they paused for breath, she began to speak, and they cut her off and resumed the yelling. She did not know how to fight a room full of voices.

That day became many days.

They lived in one big house with many rooms, but one kitchen. She had to enter that kitchen to cook, to drink water, to function. Every time their eyes met her, the shouting began again. No one hit her. But words can bruise in ways the body remembers.

Her sleep disappeared. Nightmares replaced rest. Exhaustion made everything louder in her mind. Even then, she tried to stay silent for her son's sake.

And then came the night.

She came into the kitchen. Their eyes caught her. The insults started again. She asked one question, why they were doing this to her.

That one sentence punctured their ego. The shouting started to double.

The night was warm, silent, and dark, but inside the house, voices crashed over her from every side. No one softened. No one stepped in. Days without sleep had scraped her raw; her body shook with exhaustion, her mind breaking under the pressure.

Then her eyes caught the knife.

She grabbed it before she could think, before she could remember her son who had been sleeping beside her only minutes ago.

Slash, slash, slash, slash…

Thirteen quick cuts across her left arm in the blink of an eye, an attempt to silence the storm.

After the hospital

Her father came to the hospital furious and broken. He wanted to take his daughter and grandson home for a few days, until the tension settled. Before leaving, he acted on his anger. He blamed his son-in-law for what had happened, for the fact that his daughter was in a hospital bed. And in that anger, he did something small that later became "big" in their eyes: he folded his hands and thanked his son-in-law for bringing her to the hospital, a bitter thank-you, sharp with accusation.

The son-in-law took it personally.

That offence hardened into a decision: he would leave her.

Divorce was mentioned. She was told it was coming.

Painkillers gave her sleep for a few days. When she came back to herself, guilt crushed her. She regretted risking her life. She regretted what could have happened to her son, to her parents. She didn't want to die. She had only wanted the pain to stop.

Meanwhile, her husband repeated the folded-hands gesture to his parents and sister. They turned it into a story of disrespect. They became afraid to let her back in.

Her sister-in-law said, "It's good she cut herself. What if she had stabbed me?"

And again, she was called a psycho.

All of them sided against her. They voted for divorce, and that night, it was decided.

Her voice now

"Relax. I am not divorced," I say today. "I'm living a happy life now."

After that incident, my husband and my in-laws did threaten divorce. For some days, there was no communication from them at all. I spoke to friends and advisors. Many told me, "Leave. Get divorced. Live your own life."

But how could I? I had a son who loved his father. What answer would I give him?

I knew I could protect myself, and protect my parents, by staying away. But I also wanted a normal life for my child. And I still loved my husband. He is an innocent man, easily influenced. If his parents could influence him with cruelty, I wanted to pull him back with my love.

So, I waited. There were conversations. There were negotiations. I apologized. My father apologized too. After much begging, I was taken back.

Nothing changed immediately. The insults returned. The fights returned. I stayed patient. I did not argue back. I cried silently. The only hands that wiped my tears were mine, and sometimes my little son's.

Slowly, very slowly, my husband noticed what I had been enduring. At first, he supported me quietly. Then he supported me openly. Eventually, he began fighting for me in front of his parents and sister.

I continued caring for my in-laws. Over time, my father-in-law softened. Later, my mother-in-law came to accept me more. My sister-in-law remained cold, especially when we met in the same kitchen, but life became bearable.

Today, my husband takes great care of me. We had a second son. And gradually, even the grandparents and his aunt began loving him too.

I could have avoided the discomfort and the trouble by choosing the easy way out. I could have taken revenge. But I am not built like that. I do not know how to fight with hate, I only know how to fight for love. I could have listened to everyone. I could have accepted divorce and survived. But I wanted to fight for my marriage, for the father of my son. I believed my pain was worth it, so I endured.

Now I am healing. My parents are happy. My home is calmer than it was. The scars on my arm remain. They will not heal. They will tell my story.

And if I can share one message with anyone living a similar story, I will say it plainly: if the pain is worth it, endure it. Fight for your marriage. I thought my pain was worth it, so I did.

6 THE MOTHER AFTER MATERNITY LEAVE

It is the last night of her five-month maternity leave.

Tomorrow morning, she must go back to work.

The house is quiet. The fan turns. Her baby sleeps. But inside her head, nothing is quiet. Anxiety keeps circling the same thought: I must leave my baby.

Her mother-in-law will be home, yes, but she is old. Will she have energy after lunch? Will she notice the baby's cues the way a mother does? Will the baby accept being fed by her? Will she change the diaper on time? Will the baby be safe if she starts moving around, rolling, reaching, and fussing?

The questions do not stop. They grow. And without her realizing, morning arrives.

She does not need the alarm. She turns it off before it rings and gets up like she must, because she is a mother, and mothers move even when they feel broken inside.

She cooks lunch for herself and her husband, packs it neatly in a tiffin, and leaves it on the kitchen table. She takes a hot bath and gets ready for work, careful with every sound so she does not wake her sleeping daughter. She skips breakfast; fear has taken away her appetite.

Then comes the part she hates most: expressing milk.

They call it "expressing," as if it is nothing, just a routine. She pumps, wincing through the discomfort, fills the bottles, seals them, refrigerates them, and tells her mother-in-law when to feed the baby.

Everything for the baby is prepared: chilled milk, a mosquito-netted crib, a room that stays safe, an inverter in case the power goes out. Everything is ready, except the mother being present.

It is time to catch the office cab.

She bends over the crib and kisses her baby. Her hands tremble. Her eyes fill. She holds the baby's small, delicate fingers, not too tightly, just long enough to feel its warmth, breathe in its scent, and store it in her memory.

Then she shuts her eyes tightly, turns away, and leaves quickly before she changes her mind.

At the last second, she realizes she has forgotten her tiffin. For a moment she freezes, then forces herself to move again. Never mind. I will eat in the canteen.

In the cab, she takes the window seat. Traffic barely moves. Tears slide down her cheeks as guilt rises like a tide. The world outside looks normal. Inside her, everything feels wrong. She has done everything "right", milk, crib, safety, yet the one thing her baby wants most is the one thing she cannot leave behind: her.

At the office, people welcome her. "Welcome back!" "How's the baby?" Smiles, small talk, friendly voices. She smiles back and nods, but she feels like she has walked into a place that continued living without her. The floor looks cleaner. There are new faces. Some teammates have changed. The office feels familiar and unfamiliar at the same time.

Work begins. Emails wait. Tasks wait. Everyone looks focused.

She isn't.

Her body sits at the desk, but her heart is in the crib at home.

Lunch arrives and she remembers her tiffin is still on the kitchen table. She orders canteen food and eats without tasting it. Halfway through, she video-calls her mother-in-law.

"Did she drink the milk? Is she okay?"

Only when she hears, "She drank. She is sleeping," does her chest loosen enough to breathe.

After lunch, she returns to her desk.

The sleepless night catches her. Her eyes burn. Her head feels heavy. Coffee keeps her awake, but it does not return her focus. She tries to concentrate, but her mind keeps flashing to her baby, her tiny face, her soft sounds, the way she smells. She swears she can hear her baby even inside the office.

Her hand rests on the mouse and, without meaning to, she holds it gently, as if it is her baby's hand.

She blinks hard. Her eyes sting. She keeps working.

Part of her wants to stand up and quit immediately, rage-quit, run home, pick up her baby, and never let go.

But she needs the money. Bills do not pause for motherhood. That is the cruel truth pressing down on her: love pulling her one way, survival pulling her the other.

When the workday finally ends, she rushes into the cab, rushes home, and runs straight to the crib. The baby is sleeping, but she does not care. She lifts her up, hugs her close, and cries into her soft warmth. Relief only reaches her when her baby is against her skin again.

That night, for a few hours, she feels calm, because she is back with her baby. But as the clock moves toward 10 pm, anxiety returns. Tomorrow is another workday.

She tucks the baby in, lies down, and closes her eyes, then opens them again. She watches her baby sleep: the tiny hands, the fragile hair moving slightly under the fan. She memorizes her child as if she is afraid time will steal something from her.

She sleeps for two hours.

The baby cries.

She feeds, rocks, soothes, and settles her. She lies down again. After about 2 hours of sleep, the baby cries again, diaper, comfort, back to sleep.

By morning, she counts her sleep: four hours, broken into pieces.

Not enough, she tells herself. But better than yesterday.

She cooks breakfast and lunch for the family. She packs her tiffin carefully, and this time, before she forgets, she places it in her office bag.

Today, she feels a little fresher in the office, but the work feels harder. Emails interrupt her. Tasks feel heavier than they used to. She looks at the clock: 11 a.m. Only two hours have passed. It feels like a whole day.

She lifts her head above the monitor and looks around.

Everyone else is glued to their screens. Keyboard sounds fill the air, fast, steady, relentless. Nobody looks up. Nobody pauses. And suddenly a new fear enters her chest: They are moving like machines. I can't compete like this anymore.

She cannot "prove herself" with the same ease. She knows who will get the praise, the people who can give all of themselves to work.

Yesterday, she wanted to quit.

Today, she fears she will fall behind and lose her job. Fear, paranoia, sleeplessness, her body still recovering, her mind still healing, hormones still settling, everything pulls at her mood like a storm.

She gets irritated without warning. Irritated at her manager for assigning tasks. Irritated at teammates who come with doubts. Irritated at small sounds, small delays, small demands. The anger builds and looks for somewhere to go. For a moment, she wants to snap at someone, shout, be rude, just to release the pressure.

But she does not.

Because she knows better. She was raised to understand that pain explains you, but it does not give you the right to hurt others. So, she swallows it, steadies her voice, and carries it quietly, like she carries everything else.

With all the doubts going on in her own mind, she forces herself to focus. She repeats the same sentence in her mind like a prayer: My baby is safe. I must work.

At lunch, she video calls again, hears that the baby is fine, and returns to her desk. She concentrates with all her might and pushes through the afternoon. She could not complete her tasks for the day, so has to stay back to complete them. Before motherhood, extra hours felt normal. Now, extra hours feel like time stolen from her baby. She cannot stay late the way others can. So, she decides to take her work laptop home to finish incomplete tasks.

She rushes home again, lifts her baby again, holds her again, and cries again.

It is only her second day back, and it already feels like she is living two lives at once. She opens her laptop with her baby on her lap, feeding at her breast while her fingers move over the keyboard. Work on the screen, motherhood in her arms, both demanding her at the same time.

And even in that moment, guilt finds her. She hates that she cannot give her baby her full, undivided attention. She is here, she is feeding, she is present, yet she still feels like she is failing because she has to do it while doing something else.

She tells herself, Three more working days, then weekend.

Wednesday, Thursday, Friday, three more days. Then two full days with her baby.

When the weekend finally arrives, joy fills her chest. There was a time when weekends meant friends, movies, shopping, new recipes, and long, relaxed plans. Now weekend means one thing: her baby, fully hers.

Weekend arrives, she's happy with her baby. Saturday was fine but on Sunday evening, her hands start trembling again, because Monday is coming.

She realizes she needs help, not advice from people who only say "be strong," but guidance from someone who has lived this exact life before.

So, she takes her baby and goes to her senior colleague's house. She trusts this woman can lend her confidence, because she has lived it, postpartum, maternity leave, and the return to work, not once, but twice. Her children are teenagers now. At work, she is respected, considered one of the best, and known for managing time with ease. She has done all of it, and survived the same storm.

The young mother sits in her home and finally lets everything spill out: the guilt, the fear, the inability to focus, the urge to quit, the fear of losing her job, the helplessness of not being able to afford staying home.

"I don't know what to do," she says. "Should I quit or continue?"

The senior colleague listens carefully. Then she says the simplest truth first:

"If you want to quit and you can afford it, quit."

But she can't afford it.

So, the colleague nods, as if she already knows, and says, "Then don't torture yourself by pretending this isn't hard."

She leans forward. "There are women who dream of the life you have," she says. "A homemaker dreams of earning so she can buy more things for her baby. The construction women you see outside, shirts over their saris, dream of an office job like yours, where maternity leave exists, and the pay still comes in when their bodies are still recovering."

She looks at her steadily. "And you dream of being rich enough to stay home with your baby without worrying about money."

Then she adds, softer but firm: "Some women earn daily wages.

They do not get maternity leave at all. They go back to work because they must, even when their bodies aren't ready, even when their hearts are still at home."

She pauses. "None of these dreams is wrong," she says. "Every woman is just trying to survive her version of love."

Then she adds gently, "And listen, you got your full maternity leave. Some women don't. Some colleagues have had complicated pregnancies and are forced to start leave early. By the time the baby is born, their leave is already half-used, and they go back to work with barely two months at home with their newborn babies."

She shakes her head. "Imagine that heartbreak."

Her voice softens. "I am not saying your pain is small. I am saying you're not alone in it, and perspective can help you breathe when guilt is choking you."

Then her voice softens. "The hard part is not loving your baby. The hard part is loving your baby while doing everything else too, sleepless nights followed by long workdays, a postpartum body still aching, a mind still storming, deadlines that don't care, and a heart that only wants to be in the crib."

The young mother's eyes fill again.

The colleague continues, steady and sure: "You think you're struggling because you gave birth. But everyone struggles after a long break. You remember our colleague who returned after months recovering from an accident? He struggles too. That is normal."

She smiles gently. "If you were good at your work before, you will find your form again. And if you were not good before, listen to me, I have seen women become far better after motherhood. Something changes after you become a mother. You learn time differently. You learn and focus differently. You learn strength differently."

Then she says the one sentence that lands like truth: "If you're crying, cry," she says. "But you will still do it. I cried too. I crossed the stage you are in right now. And now I am in a different stage, I cry about different things."

She gives a small smile, "Crying doesn't mean you're failing. Crying means you're carrying two worlds at once, and you're still showing up."

Then she adds, "My babies have grown into teenagers now and raising them isn't easy either. I never know what kind of trouble they are going to bring. They always bring different troubles. That is a different kind of struggle and that will come to you when it comes. But right now, this time, this baby-time, does not return. Babies grow faster than our hearts can accept. Do not let worry steal what you'll never get back. Be with her. Admire her. Hold her whenever you can."

The young mother listens, but her eyes drift to the woman sitting in front of her, calm, steady, composed, and envy rises in her chest. When will I become like her? she wonders. When will life stop feeling like a storm? For a moment she wishes she could skip this whole chapter and wake up in the future, already strong, already stable, already fine.

Then doubt follows quickly behind: Just because she did it does not mean I can. But her senior colleague seems to read her face. She does not lecture her or rush her, she just looks at her quietly, with the certainty only experience can give, and thinks: She will make it. All mothers do.

Because she has seen this fear before. She has lived these sleepless nights, this guilt, this shaking doubt. And she knows what comes after it, not perfection, not ease, but steadiness. A rhythm. A strength. A mother who finds her feet again.

7 THE CHILDLESS WOMAN

It was a dark summer night in a small marriage hall in a small town. Music and cheers were heard in every corner of the marriage hall, and inside, in a cramped side room, a familiar question landed like a stone in an already open wound.

"It's been seven years already. When will you and your husband bless us with a baby?" a distant relative asked, loud enough for ten others to hear in that room. This question would have hurt her even in private. But the question was not answered. All the old eyes were fixed on the only childless young woman in the room. She swallowed the shame and pain, but still managed to put on a kind smile and said softly, "We're trying, aunty." She smiled again to change the subject, protecting everyone else from that very discomfort she was experiencing. It was not the first time. Not the first aunt. Not the first gathering. The same question always found her.

She used to love family functions, the cheerful noise everywhere, joyful, familiar faces everywhere, the scent of jasmine in all the women's hair, the aroma of festival food, everything about them excited her. But all the excitement vanished a year after her wedding. Family functions quickly turned into minefields, and the thought of attending a function was a nightmare for her. Skipping them would have spared her the insults and heartache, but it would have been considered rude, so, against her own will, she forced herself to attend, and endured the uncomfortable question again and again. As

if the pregnancy-related questions were not brutal enough, sometimes, alongside those questions came "advice": try this position, try that doctor, visit this temple, that priest and this diet. As if her life were a puzzle strangers could solve in the span of a conversation.

Some people should know that babies do not appear out of thin air. There is an intimate, private process behind it, and some people just lack the decency to know they should not quiz the childless in public or in private.

Every year, every suggestion, every pointed question pushed her and her husband toward a hard decision, one that would drill into her body and spirit in pursuit of a child. With much hesitation and desperation, they chose in vitro fertilization (IVF). Most people call this "test-tube baby method", and this method, for the next 6 months, made her life hell with tests, injections, tablets and surgeries. After beginning the treatment, their savings vanished into hospital bills, but after 6 months, when she was nearly empty physically, emotionally, and financially, the doctors finally said she was ready for the intrauterine insemination - the step where prepared sperm is placed in the uterus to help conception.

In her own words:

"Daily injection in my thigh - but the good thing is I get to have the injection on a different thigh each day, so the previous day's pain has time to heal. And did I say I also take nine pills every day? Maybe it is the pills, because my stomach burns almost all the time. Before all this, the doctors did two small incisions on my stomach - a surgery I barely understood, 'preparing my body,' they said, for the pregnancy. Afterwards, I could not walk for days. Whenever I went to the restroom, I urinated blood, and my stomach was burning, and I was afraid to drink water, even in that harsh summer. So yes, maybe I am better now. 'Better' just means a different kind of pain, I guess."

She thought of her childhood, two brothers, a small house, a mother who would often say, "I carried you in my womb for ten months, and this is the respect you show me?" The world had changed. For many women, the struggle now stretched beyond ten months: months of trying, of needles, tablets, and scans, added to the months of pregnancy. Twelve months, then ten more. A long, moving target called hope.

In her own words, again:

"They will attempt implantation soon for me. Then, ten more months to carry what we have prayed for. Oh, it will be worth it, I tell myself. We have spent money we did not have. I take more tablets than meals. I see the doctor more than I see my parents. My stomach feels like it is on fire. But in the end, all this pain and effort will be worth it, won't it? And that is what matters the most, doesn't it? But to tell you the truth, none of my relatives know that we are using this artificial method to conceive. Not that this is a big secret, but then they would say my baby is not natural, and I don't want that to happen. Even if it is artificial, I just wish my baby lives a healthy and blameless life compared to mine. But again, going through all of this, I wish someone had never invented this IVF method because then adoption would be the only solution to childlessness. There are so many babies in the world who are orphaned, and if this painful but useful method had not been invented, we all could have adopted so many orphaned children. Anyway, IVF is all we have for now, so I have to go through this.

I just wish my relatives knew how much it costs, body, mind, and soul, to try to bring a baby into this world during these modern times." What they did to me - I can live with it, but I just hope they are a bit kinder to the next childless woman who enters into this family.

8 THE WORKING MOTHER

As the first alarm goes off at 5 a.m., she wakes her husband, and they begin their day. She works as a clerk at a local court in her city, and her husband is an engineer whose work starts at 5:45 am daily. Her husband's work often requires him to be on site before sunrise, so the burden of getting their kindergartner son to school fell on her. After sending her husband off to work at 5:30 am, she cooks breakfast and lunch for their son, her husband and herself. When the second alarm goes off at 6 a.m., it is time for her to do the next most challenging task: wake their son up, get him ready, and make him breakfast, all in 1 hour. There is one universal truth - the first five school years for a child's parents are always the hardest. Their kids will not know how to brush, bathe, or eat, and even if they did learn, they don't want to go to school. Mostly, their mother must help them do these things and get them ready. Children being children are cranky, crying, and careless, but their mother can't afford to be like that. She knows education and food are essential for her child's future. So, with much struggle, she beats the clock, gets her kid ready, skips her own breakfast, and waits for her husband outside her house to drop their son off at school, then later drops her off at her office.

Not even halfway through the day, she is tired from all the stress and work she's done since early morning. There is one satisfaction for her, though - that she made her son reach school on time, gave him and her husband their lunch and snack boxes. All her household responsibilities were done for the morning, and now it was time for her to pray that her son would not get into trouble at school or start a new one. The last thing she wanted was her son's schoolteacher calling to inform her about an incident involving her son. Nevertheless, nothing had happened to her son, so she now had to complete all her office work on time so she could be available for her son early in the evening. She was super productive and super-efficient. When all her colleagues took the time to talk and go on breaks during work, she was extremely productive and efficient. She was hard on herself, taking no breaks during working hours, and worked even while having lunch. All her colleagues admired her, and often they would jokingly ask her why she was working so hard; all she could think of was her family. She knows she can take it easy a little bit, but behind all this extra struggle is a reason. The reason to gain back what she lost during her maternity leave - plenty of work to do, plenty of catching up to do, proving to do and getting the promotion so she can provide better for her family.

The day ended, and although she was disciplined and efficient, unlike anyone else there, she still could not complete all her tasks, so she once again took the work home, stayed up late, and finished it later that night.

Struggling with strained, sleepy eyes, she cooks dinner for her family, feeds her son, and puts him to sleep. After her husband and son slept, and all the noise had settled, leaving only the silence of the night and the chirping of crickets, she resumed her office work and began fishing at 1 a.m. As she crawls to her bed for a much-deserved rest, she feels relieved - a day gone well without any incidents, but deep inside, she cries for help. Although she loves her son and adores his tiny size, she can't wait for him to grow up so he can take care of himself a little, allowing her some time to rest. Then she thinks of her own mother and looks up to her as her inspiration. She remembers how her mother must have struggled to raise her and her two brothers single-handedly when she was a child. She compares herself with other good parents. There are parents who struggle financially but still send their kids to school, and there are parents who are sick but still provide for their children. Compared to them, her struggles are nothing; she felt and went to sleep. As the morning dawned, the first alarm went off at 5 a.m., and she woke up with her husband to begin their next day.

9 The HOMEMAKER

On a gloomy winter day in London, a young boy who had come to a strange new country to study stayed in a two-bedroom apartment with his friends. While cooking for himself and his friends, he accidentally cut his finger while chopping onions for the biriyani he planned to cook that day. Although it was just a small cut with a blunt knife, it bothered him every time water touched the open wound. In a bachelor's room where responsibilities were shared, he spoke to his friends and said he would not be cooking or cleaning for the next 4 days until his finger cut healed. His friends were kind enough to agree to his request and happily shared the extra chores amongst themselves. The boy now had little to do, and his friends prepared food for him. The biriyani he was supposed to prepare was taken over by his friends, and he was served it hot. As he happily ate the biriyani and lay down to rest that afternoon, he realized that was the first time he hadn't worked for his food ever since he came to London. The relaxation took him back to the times when his mom used to cook food for him when he was in India with her. Delving deeper into his memories, he could only remember his mom cooking for him and could not think of anyone else who cooked at his house while he was a kid. This later took him back to his school days, when he used to wake up at 6 o'clock, 1 hour after his mother. In a family of four, the boy and his brother studied in the same school, where their father worked as a teacher. As a result, the mother, a homemaker, was responsible for cooking breakfast and lunch for all three of them. Although the childhood flashbacks brought him a little joy, he could not help but decide to be a little less selfish and wonder about his mother.

In all those 25 years in India with his mother, he never once remembered thinking that his mother might also have cuts on her hands while cooking, just like him. In fact, his mother always had to cook quickly, which meant chopping vegetables quickly. The process would have involved many accidental cuts and burns, but he never once remembered his dad buying food from a restaurant or from the school canteen for them. There was always fresh, homemade, healthy, warm food for him, his brother, and his father. He now remembered that his father never took a single sick day from work, and that his mother never took a sick day from family responsibilities. She was always at work - early in the morning and late at night. He realized why he remembered his mother always yawning. Those yawns were cries for sleep - a little rest. Back in his days, they weren't financially well and washing machines were still a rarity in many Indian houses so his mother washed everyone's clothes by hand. She was always at work so her family wore clean clothes. His mother was highly religious and fasted for the betterment of the family, 5 out of 7 days a week. However, there was always food available three times a day for the rest of the family members. No matter who ate non-veg in the house, she fasted and prepared for them.

As a kid, he didn't have the knowledge and experience to help his dad with his work, but at least he could have helped his mom with the dishes. He wished someone were there to advise him on how to help his mother, or that someone had already told him, but for his age, he must have ignored it. Either way, a mistake was made, and although it was committed many times over many years, the realization hit him only when he was away from his mother. Panicking over the mistake he made in all those 25 years by not asking his mother if she needed any help, he wanted to correct his mistake now, but it is too late, for he's in his late 20s and his mother is in her late 50s.

As a below-average student, he often heard his dad scream at him, "I'm working this hard only for you to study well", but not once did he hear his mother complain.

All she knew was to nurture her kids and make them healthy and happy. "When I get married and have my own kids, I will never let my wife go through what my mother went through because of me," the boy said to himself. The boy is now grown up and washes his own dishes, cooks his own food, but he wishes he could be with his mother now to help her with her chores. Separated by distance and past mistakes, all he can do is wait to return to his mother so he can take his turn caring for her.

While the boy was going through this roller coaster of memories and emotions in a cold, cloudy island - on the other sunny side of the world, was the boy's mother, not remembering a single sacrifice she made for him, who picks up her phone to call her son to check if he ate on time or not.

10 THE SINGLE WORKING WOMAN

The girl from another town finished all her office work for the day and was getting ready to leave, since it was already 7:00 pm. As she was getting ready, a male colleague approached her and asked where she lived and if he could drop her off.

"No, thank you. I live in my uncle's house, and his sons, my nephews, will ask me a lot of questions if I go home with friends," said the girl from a different town. The male colleague then left her alone, and the girl travelled not to her uncle's house, but to her ladies' hostel. The truth is, there were no uncles or brothers. She was all alone in that strange town. She was there to work, and although she was alone, she was smart to tell everyone that she lived with people who would be there for her if something went wrong. This shrewdness was not inherent; it was a skill she developed. Frequent unwanted advances, beginning in her youth, taught her to craft elaborate lies, a necessary defense against those who tried to take advantage of her isolated life. Already coming from a small town, the girl worked in a town just a little bigger than hers.

The company she worked for was run by bad managers, and it had poor policies and limited rights for women. When her parents tried their best to find her a suitable groom, she did not find one, and that continued until she turned 30. At work in a different hometown, she was being approached by her teammates and colleagues inappropriately. In her hometown, her relatives and neighbors spoke badly of her. Every parent deserves to speak to their children at least once a day, but the pressure from their relatives made them put some of that pressure on her. Almost every conversation they had involved her getting married soon. This made her sometimes skip speaking to them.

Nevertheless, she concentrated on her work even in a toxic workplace; she developed skills and contributed positively to her team, which was hostile toward her. She built professionalism in a place that had less of it. An unmarried 30-year-old woman at the office drew unwarranted negative attention, creating a hostile environment among her colleagues and teammates. And once every month, her own body contributed to the distress that her work and personal life brought her - her dysmenorrhea made it extremely difficult for her to sleep, eat and work properly. Excruciating pain, sleepless nights, and the resulting mood swings severely hampered her ability to perform at her best at work. Nevertheless, she did not let her own hardships spoil someone else's day.

"My upbringing taught me better, so I will never let my menstruating body and its resulting mood swings unjustly transfer my pain to someone who is innocent" - her words paraphrased.

She was kind, compassionate, and professional to all her colleagues who deserved it.

Her struggles and carefully acquired virtues and skills have made her who she is today. The single working woman later married a good man, has two handsome sons now, and works in a larger city at a larger company than she did in her former town and job. Even though she's completely switched to a new and better career now, she knows for a fact that she wouldn't have got this job if it weren't for the good qualities she acquired in her early career.

11 THE SPORTS WOMAN

She is one of the most childish, talkative, naughty, and at the same time confident, people anyone could meet on a football field. With fire in her words and ambition in her eyes, she can convince anyone to join her team. This is the story of a young girl who will become a football sensation.

"I was born in a small coastal town. I'm the only daughter of my parents. We are not rich, not even middle-class. My dad is an auto driver, and my mother sells fish near the sea. Still, my parents put me in a private school for one reason and one reason only: like many others, we have some toxic relatives who look down on us every time. My parents wanted me to get a good education, find a white-collar job, and be in a respectable position so we could be respected among our relatives.

But my interest was not in a white-collar job.

We had Physical Education every week in school, and when all the boys and girls picked up cricket balls, I picked up a football. The first time I touched a football, at seven years old, I instantly knew that this game would be my life. In the lower classes, my parents were very supportive. Most parents put their daughters in karate to learn self-defense; I convinced mine to put me in football so I could build stamina, strength, and flexibility. To my surprise, they agreed. After that, I worked hard, learned new skills and tricks, and tried to learn everything there is to know about football. I am not good at cooking. I am not shy like other girls. I am not great at math. I am not even what people call "beautiful." I am not even good at being a girl, I know that. But the one thing I am good at, the one thing I am confident about, is football. Football is my life. As I grew up, I won many inter- and intra-school matches. I aspire to play for the national team one day and make my country proud. I want to play in the Olympics too, I hope our country qualifies soon. Cricket was once like football in our country; one World Cup made it a religion. In the same way, I will win many games for our country, and football will become big.

I'm a confident girl, just a little less than before. When people say I talk too much, I laugh and tell them they should have met me three years ago; my mouth was even bigger then.

Two things trimmed that edge.

First: we trained like mad for a match. I had even rehearsed some goal celebrations, something fun for the crowd when I scored. But our energy leaked out before kickoff. The "crowd" waiting to watch the match was just our boyfriends. Not even our parents came. The actual crowd drifted to the men's game happening on the same day and at the same time in a football field just a few feet away from our field. I even heard a couple of women say, "Let's watch the men's game, it'll be faster, more interesting." That day did to me what no defender ever has.

Second: the same parents who cheered for me when I was little have started to pull me back. Relatives whisper timelines, get her married as soon as college ends. Some even joke that they should hurry before I "break my legs" in a match.

Put together, it stings. But I'm still here, lacing up, letting the hurt turn into hunger.

Most parents who enroll their daughters in sports think it is cute at first. They do not do it dreaming of their daughters winning national medals. When we grow up, many parents say it is time to focus on "serious" things rather than sports. But sport is serious, for us sportswomen, it is a calling. I have watched many sports and army films; I salute the soldiers who fall on foreign soil without even a proper burial. In the army, they say true honor isn't the medal, it's the sacrifice you make for the country that matters the most. In our small way, athletes who play for the country live by a similar principle. If we make it, we bring medals for the country. If we do not, a few years later, you might find us selling fish or fruit on the street. But even then, there is a quiet satisfaction: we tried for our country, and if we failed, at least we failed in its service. For athletes like us, with no big name, no safety net, no rich family, adversity is our fuel.

It is hard even to form a team. Our coach struggled like us when she was young, she tells us her stories and reminds us to keep fighting for the game we love. With a lot of effort, she and I have brought in new players. Every time we think we finally have good chemistry in the team, we lose players one by one. Some girls say they cannot handle the pressure from their parents; some say they are getting married and leaving town; most just stop coming without a word. I have played with many players, both young and old. We even have women in their thirties. After childbirth, I see them struggle; once brilliant players can seem like newbies, as if they have never touched a ball in their life. But I appreciate their husbands who bring them and drop them on the ground. Seeing all that, my coach says the country has changed a lot and is now more supportive of women's sports. I know there's still a long way to go, but if my coach says that, I believe her time was even harder.

As a sportswoman, I am facing many struggles. I can manage mine, but seeing my parents struggle because I love this game breaks my heart. My relatives make fun of them, insult them, and even scold them for letting me be like this. If I do not have the skills and my game isn't good, I'll leave the sport and find a full-time job. But saying I should stop playing just because I am a woman? - Now that really hurts! Mostly, football has two halves. If the opponent scores two goals in the first half, they act like the game is theirs. But if we come back in the second half and equalize, you can see fear in their eyes, from the strikers right up to the goalkeeper. And if we go on to win, that is a true comeback. That's the kind of comeback I want in front of my relatives. If I can win in front of them, there would be no greater satisfaction for me. Through my game, I want to show my relatives and neighbors what our family is capable of.

One good thing about football is you can play it in pretty much any condition, indoors, outdoors, summer, winter, even in the rain. I love playing in the rain; it changes how the ball lands, swerves, and bounces. I do not get much time, so I wake up early and do my workouts. I can catch up on training by sacrificing sleep, but some things don't come easily, like protein. We struggle to get enough because we are poor. Protein helps you get stronger and build stamina. I wish I could get more and become a better player. I do not want free money. Most girls my age get pocket money from their parents; I stopped taking it long ago. I sell fish with my mother and earn a little. For now, it's enough.

Football tells a lot about a person. Scoring goals is a big part of football. You score, the crowd chants your name, that is the ultimate glory for us small players. So, everyone is hungry to score. When you take the ball near the goalpost with much struggle and luck, and when there are no defenders near you and only the goalkeeper is between you and the net, you want the glory shot. But do not let your emotions cheat you because at that time, your judgment gets cloudy; your mind tricks you to think you can do the impossible. You will be selfish and want to score a difficult goal yourself. But usually, all the defenders rush to the one with the ball, and the teammate who is free from defenders near you has the better chance of scoring. Whether you try the shot yourself or pass it to your teammate at that important time shows not only your game sense but also your character. Anyone who chooses to pass the ball rather than take the selfish shot is my friend. That is how I pick my friends on the field.

I am doing everything I can to reach the national team. I play for my college side and enter local tournaments, sometimes guesting for other teams when the rules allow. I'm trialing for my state squad and for clubs that compete in the Indian Women's League, because strong performances there and at the Senior Women's National Football Championship are the usual pathways to national selection. National camps are invitation-only through the AIFF, so my focus is on earning that call-up through performances, fitness tests, and consistent form.

I am from South India and don't speak much Hindi, the most widely spoken language in the country. Selection is based on football, not language, but I am still learning Hindi to communicate better with coaches, teammates, and the media. Once, I did not know football either; I learned it. I will learn this, too, for the game I love.

Many sports lovers start with dreams, but when nothing works, they join gyms as trainers or become PT teachers in schools. I do not like that. It is like loving someone and then marrying someone else because you couldn't get the love of your life. I am 100% confident I will play for our country one day. But with all the politics around sports and among coaches, if they do not select me because of my color, my appearance, my caste, my language, or even the food I eat, what choice will I have? I may also have to become a PT teacher in a nearby school. But that will not be my story. I am going to win and make you all proud.

Thanks to my parents, I have a unique name. When I make our country proud, I will see parents naming their daughters after me.

12 THE SOON-TO-BE DIVORCED

The heroine of this story was called "south Indian" in school and "north girl" at home. Her father's transfer had carried the family from the southern part of India all the way to Jharkhand, and that is where most of her childhood unfolded, steel-grey mornings, Hindi on her tongue, mustard oil in her hair, and an easy, outgoing attitude just like any other girl for her age. She was the youngest of three, first a sister, then a brother, and then her, forever the last to be scolded and the first to be forgiven. Right from a young age, she was told what to do and what to expect - and she followed it. By doing so, she had a perfectly happy and normal childhood while she was in school, but then came the time when she had to go to the next part of her life.

It was time for her to start her college life, and so her parents steered her back south. She was told to go to Chennai, to a university her parents trusted and a city where her relatives could "keep an eye." Her parents didn't want their youngest to eat outside food or learning the loneliness of hostel life. Money would be sent every month; they promised the relatives. "Treat her like your own," was all they asked of them, and for a while, she tried to believe they did.

Dreams unpacked themselves quietly in that new house of her relatives', but the kitchen told the truth. Meals arrived undercooked or scant; some nights, they didn't arrive at all. She said nothing. She convinced herself not to tell her parents, as it might worry them. "It'll be fine" became a daily prayer for her.

In the absence of parents, and their affection, a girl's next best shelter is her best friend's shoulder. Therefore, she confided in her college best friend. She was fortunate because, for her, he was the kind of friend who listened more than he spoke. For the story's sake, let's call this friend "Rolex". Rolex noticed the tremor in her voice and the lightness in her frame. No true friend sleeps well after learning a friend has gone hungry. The next morning, a lunchbox was found on her desk. Then another. And another, day after day, semester after semester. Rolex convinced his mom to cook for the heroin too during weekdays. And on weekends, when there was no college, he introduced her to his parents and made her visit his home on weekdays. In his home, food came hot, care came easy, and no one asked for anything in return. The young heroine, once alone and hungry, found herself held by a good friend's family, and by their better food.

Only then did she tell her parents the truth: the trusted relatives, the bad food, the slow humiliation. They were wounded to hear it, but relieved she was safe now, grateful for Rolex and his family, who had fed her without asking her to shrink.

Friendship, when it is real, moves patiently. The heroine had Rolex walk her to bus stops, wait outside exam halls, and their friendship gradually grew into love. Their families met; jokes were traded across living rooms; he travelled with her to Jharkhand during a semester break and greeted her parents in careful Tamil and easier smiles. Though they were not engaged, they were merely sure.

Then, without warning, a boulder fell: diabetes. He thought he was too young for it. He did not just love her, he respected her. That love and that respect would not let his sick self-stand beside the angel of his life. He told himself not to be selfish by marrying a "perfect" girl. He told himself he would not want his own daughter to marry someone unwell like him. So, Rolex asked for a breakup.

She said the diabetes did not matter to her. He decided it did. He wanted her to have "the best," and in his fear, he ruled himself out, gently and firmly. Once again, the heroine was told what to do in her life; she obeyed. She accepted his decision, and they broke up.

But kindness does not break on command. He still brought her food every day. She still visited his parents. Their families, too entangled to separate, continued to treat one another like in-laws without a wedding. It hurt to be "just friends", and they did it anyway, with the steady resilience of people who care more about each other's well-being than about tidy labels.

Things moved fast afterwards, and they graduated. The world, as it does, drew a straight line toward the next ritual.

In many Indian homes, a daughter's degree is followed by a wedding invitation. Hers were no exception. Her parents found a groom who checked all the boxes: good family, good job, good standing. She noticed different things: village values in a town address; rules about what a woman should wear; a house where a daughter-in-law would be defined by the weight of her chores.

She voiced her fears, but her parents, anxious not to lose a "good alliance," told her to trust them. And so, being told what to do again, she tried trusting them. Calls were exchanged; compatibility was not. Almost 100% sure the marriage would not work out, she wanted to stop the wedding but couldn't, as the date was already set and the invitations had been printed and handed out to relatives and friends.

There was nothing left but to accept her fate and pray she could come to terms with it. The wedding happened. The first night did not. She told her husband they were still getting to know each other and that she needed time before intimacy. He agreed, at least in words.

In a house where privacy was thin, she slept on the floor, and he slept on the bed. He never forced himself on her, but he chose a different cruelty: every morning he woke before her and left the bedroom door wide open so his parents and sisters could see "how their son was being denied." Day after day, the open door told the same story, she on the floor, he on the bed. The scolding began. The cursing followed. Though she was not ready to share a bed, she cooked, cleaned, and kept the house. Still, they called her ungrateful and pressed her harder. Although he never laid a hand on her, one thing always frightened her. Some nights she would wake for no reason and, in the dark of their locked bedroom, between 2 and 5 a.m., find him sitting up, staring at her without a word. It happened often enough that sleep left her for good. In that house, sleepless nights became a way of life for her.

From her in-laws, when pressure failed, punishment arrived. She was first restricted from leaving the house. To bend her will, she was later forbidden even to leave her room. She still did not accept her husband in bed. Severity increased - food portions reduced. Then, soon, even the little food she received completely vanished.

Two continuous days without food broke the seal of her silence. The heroine phoned her sister and told her about all the cruelty being inflicted on her. She cried to her sister that in that entire house, she had no one to help her. Although the heroine's sister lived in the same state felt helpless. She did not know how to help her baby sister, who was kept hostage and left hungry. At that time, the heroine's sister remembered the one person who had never let her go hungry. He was the only person who loved her so much that he broke his own heart by leaving her, just so she could be happy. The heroine's sister called him - luckily, with Rolex, she did not need much explaining to do. "What is the address?" was all he asked, and "get ready I'm on my way" was all he said. He was ready to save the love of his life.

Rolex, along with the heroin's sister, drove to the heroin's husband's house. At first, they requested them nicely to send the heroin with them. But the in-laws dismissed them at the gate. They then tried quarrelling - it did not work either. So, they went to the police and returned with enough authority to open any door. The heroine walked out with what she had arrived with: her dignity and the people who truly loved her.

Home again among family, but there, she met a different kind of pressure. "What will the neighbors say?" her parents fretted. "How long can a married daughter stay here without her husband?" She cried, then stood her ground. After days of begging her parents not to send her into that cruel house, her parents agreed that she needed a divorce. A clean end to a bad choice. At first, she believed justice would be swift. It was not. She alleged coercion and starvation; they responded with a lie, an affair with someone. Heartbroken, accused of something she would never do and insulted - she understood the divorce process would be the toughest battle she had ever faced in her life. But little did she know that while she was getting ready for a long, hard, and expensive battle, Rolex, the hero of this story, was getting ready to speak to the heroine's sister - to discuss something important - something life changing for both him and the heroine. While the heroine's sister was in suspense about what Rolex was going to ask her, he politely asked, "Could I marry her once she got her divorce?"

13 THE DIVORCED WOMAN

One hard kick to the stomach sent her crashing to the ground. She did not shout; she did not scream. Her husband, who kicked her to the ground, did that for her. Until his shouting, it was just a silent 2:00 am in their house, but his noise woke her dad, who was sleeping in the nearby room. The old father was struck with shock in the middle of the night and then later with heartbreak when he came out of the room and saw his daughter lying on the ground in pain. To spare her father the upset of her unfortunate situation, she quickly hid her pain and got back on her feet. Very soon, a quarrel broke out, "How can you hit my daughter?" asks the father, combined with both pain and anger. "Mind your business when you're in my house!" says the son-in-law, and between them, she does her best to calm them both down with eyes pouring with tears. After several minutes, when the quarrelling stopped, she convinced her father to go back to their hometown first thing in the morning. He wished he could take her home with her. She wished she could go with him. But as a devotee of Sita and Draupadi, she knew she had chosen to stay with her husband, not abandon him in that condition. She waited for dawn to break so she could get her father on the first train in the morning and travel 1100 kilometers back home.

Morning came, and so did the first train. As the train arrived, it was soon preparing to leave. The old father sat in the train near the window. Tears filled both their eyes - the father worried how his daughter would handle such a man all by herself in a faraway place from home, far from relatives and friends. The only known person in that big city where no one spoke their language was her husband, and her father had just seen him abuse her. The trains in our country may not arrive on time, but they never wait for loved ones to finish saying their goodbyes. Such was this train, unaware of the emotional exchange between the father and daughter, ready to depart.

The train was picking up speed - she walked with the train when it was slow at first. The noise it made was increasing as it sped. The train was leaving, heartbeats rising for both, as the train picked up speed. The daughter first walked as fast as she could to keep up with the speeding train- then she ran trying to keep up, but very soon they could not see each other anymore. The train's tail was all that was visible to that girl who was standing alone in that train station - the train's noise had completely gone, and it was just silence for her.

That was the last time she saw her father alive. Stress, anxiety and blood pressure, and worry about his daughter killed him. Hearing the news, she travelled 1100 kilometers back to her hometown - crying all the way, travelling through the same route her father had travelled just a few weeks ago. Even during that painful and helplessly long trip, her soul was as pure as water, never once blamed her husband for being the reason for her father's quick demise.

She arrived at her hometown, paid her last respects to her father and stayed with her widowed mother and younger brother for a few days. She mourned her father for some days in her hometown, and it was time for her to make a long, lonely trip back to her husband again. With her husband once again in that far, far away city, it was abuse once again - it was like walking on eggshells for her every day - she didn't know when he would get angry or when he would hit her again. Every day and every night were nightmares for her. As days passed, his condition got worse, and she could no longer handle him - the worst thing was that he could no longer handle himself either. One morning, when it was too much for them both to handle, she called her husband's father and mother to inform them about his condition - they travelled all the way to take their son home. She tagged along with them and stayed in their house to take care of her husband.

But he would not let her share his room. In her own husband's house, she was being treated like a guest - only she did not get the respect a guest would receive. Again, days passed, and her husband's condition became bad to worse, and he demanded that she leave their house and go back to her mom's house. At that point, it was too hard to control him, so the girl who did whatever she was told to do did that too. She left her husband for a few days and stayed with her mother in her town. Every day she would keep calling her in-laws and ask if she could come back. Every time she would get the same answer - that their son was still sick and that they would get back to her. At that time, she did not realize that she was already heading for a divorce. Somehow, she waited eight long years for her husband to get better, and he never got better. Although she was waiting, she never wasted a moment during her 8 years away from her husband. She worked, earned some money, ran her small family with her mother and younger brother, and gained some work experience.

Of course, it all came at a steep price. Some bad men in her workplace tried to exploit her, knowing her lonely situation. However, with a spirit as strong as a mountain, she never gave in to such men and stayed faithful to her husband. When the bad things that came from bad men were too much for her to handle, she would often go to the local temple to find peace. The priest, who was friendly with her after knowing her estrangement from her husband, tried to exploit her, too. Feeling forsaken by both God and colleagues, she worked from home most of the time. There came a time when her relatives and her family got impatient with her.

Every year, their impatience grew heavier as she aged, and it was time for her younger brother to marry, too. Unfortunately, in that small family without a father, being bundled with a daughter who did not live with her husband made it impossible for her brother to marry. Holding Sita and Draupadi as her inspiration, she resisted divorce as much as she could, but her voice was powerless amid the din her relatives and family raised. Their plan was to get her divorced first, then remarry her to another person, so her brother could marry.

She resisted for months and gave her relatives a hard time. "Why are you still refusing to leave him even after all these years?" they asked. No answer from her. "Has he called at least once in these 8 years?" they added. She still did not answer. Not that she could not, but she knew she would be interrupted and silenced.

After countless counseling by her relatives, she yielded reluctantly and started the divorce process. Not for herself, but for her younger brother, who still hadn't started his life because of his sister. The divorce process drained her already low money and dragged on for 1 year. When even mutual divorces are difficult to obtain, it made it extremely hard for her to receive her divorce because her husband never attended any of the court's hearings. In between all this were her relatives and her lawyer, motivating her to get a high compensation from her husband for the 8 years he wasted in her life. They asked her to cite abuse, denying pleasure and desertion for years and demand hefty compensation as her husband's family were rich. Among some bad women who suck the blood out of their husbands, there was this angel who stood as firm as a mountain and said she would not receive a single rupee from him. Although everything they asked her to cite in compensation was true, to her, he was still her husband, and she did not want him to bow his head in shame in court by publicly announcing these. A true admirer of Sita and Draupadi indeed! Continuously asked by her mother and relatives why she was throwing away an opportunity like this. The compensation money would help her get remarried. Continuously being asked "why," she finally spoke up, "Because before his own mind deceived him, he was a normal person. He was a gentleman. Although socially, he was from an upper-class, wealthy family, he still agreed to marry a lower-middle-class girl like her. He convinced his parents to cover all the wedding expenses, and he received not a penny in dowry. All these unfortunate things happened some months after her wedding, and whatever he did was beyond his control. He did not smoke or drink. He used to be generous and responsible before his own mind gave up on him. I cannot hold him responsible for what he did without his own consciousness."

Another hearing came, another no-show from her husband. But his parents came in his place. They explained to the judge all about their son's mental health and their struggle for years, and that it would be best if their daughter-in-law got a divorce and focused on her life at least from now on. She then got the divorce they had been fighting for nearly 1.5 years.

Divorce did not immediately bring her happiness and peace. The only difference now is that she was unofficially divorced before and is officially divorced now. Some bad men still made their advances, and of course, she dealt them all with her left hand. Now, with the word 'divorced' stamped on her life, her relatives pressed for a second marriage, and she had no other excuses left to refuse remarriage. No one truly understands how nervous a woman, already traumatized by a failed first marriage, feels when she is asked to remarry, fearing it will fail too.

Nevertheless, life had to go on. She was not rich - up until this day, she still isn't, but through that divorce, she didn't want to take money that wasn't hers. Instead, she trusted the education her late father had given her. She trusted her experience and hard work. 2 years after her divorce, after many struggles, she remarried a good man and now lives a peaceful life, still like Sita and Draupadi.

14 THE DIVORCED MOTHER

They say the truth is stranger than fiction. But in my life, truth is more disgusting than fiction, it really is. I will tell you a bizarre story, my own life's story, , and I hope you don't feel sick after hearing it.

I got married at a young age. At first, like every other girl, I did not want to get married at all, but the groom my father and mother chose for me was rich, handsome, and, at the same time, a good man. Who would not say no to such a marriage? So, I agreed. He took great care of me, and we loved each other. Married life was like a dream for me. Most married couples used to live with the husband's parents back then, but I lived with my husband in a different town because of his work. As I said, it was all like a dream for me. I became pregnant very soon and had my first daughter. Things were going fine, and about two years later, I had a son. Throughout both pregnancies, my mother came to the town where we were staying and cared for me. With my mother's help, I delivered both my babies successfully. My husband, my daughter, my son, and I were living happily. A typical happy family, right? Well, the happiness quickly ended after I got pregnant for the third time.

Not many people had phones back then, so I wrote my mother a letter to share the good news about my third pregnancy. To this day, I feel bad about sending that letter, because it marked my doom. As soon as my mother received it, she sent my younger sister to help me during my pregnancy. Soon, it was just my younger sister, my husband, my pregnant self, my son, and my daughter living in a single house. Very soon, I came to know about their affair. I was six months pregnant with my third baby. While my baby was still inside me, my husband, the man I loved from the bottom of my heart, had an affair with my sister. My own sister, my blood, was part of it. It has been 37 years since this happened, and I still can't accept or digest this fact.

I confronted my husband and begged him to stop the affair with my sister, but he did not listen. Although disgusting, he was a man from another house, so I told myself it was understandable that he would not listen to me, whom he had known for years by then. So, I begged my sister to leave the house and stop the affair with my husband. I promised I would forget and forgive whatever she had done; all I asked was that she leave at once. But my own sister did not listen to me either. I kept this a secret because I wanted to hold on to the good life I thought I had. Even if not for me, I wanted to be with my husband because my children needed a father. I did not want the world to criticize my children because of their father's adulterous habits. Of course, I cannot blame my ex-husband alone for that, my sister was equally to blame. But when neither my husband nor my sister was ready to listen, I remembered the two people who would help me: my father and mother.

I knew I could not explain all this to my parents through a letter, so I wanted to visit them in person. I was seven months pregnant at the time, but I travelled back to my hometown, carrying my young daughter (age 4) and son (age 2), to take this matter to my parents and convince them to talk sense into my sister and bring her back so I could resume my family life with my then-husband. After explaining everything, I brought my parents back to my husband's house to confront him and my sister together. To my astonishment, my parents did not want to help me. It was very strange to me, because they, too, tried to convince me to share my man with my younger sister. Although it was bizarre, I understood why they did that to me. We were a poor family, and my husband supported my family whenever needed by sending money orders. Money orders were a thing back then, now you have bank transfers and UPI payments, but back then, people could send money by letter. Anyway, my parents did not want to lose the cash flow they got from my husband. Moreover, they had tried to arrange my younger sister's marriage, but it was financially difficult for them, and many suitors kept rejecting her. This affair my sister had with my husband only made things easy for my parents. They thought they could marry her to my husband as well, with my acceptance.

The parents whom I brought to my husband's house, instead of convincing him to leave his bad ways and lead a good family life with me, started to advise me to accept this disgusting affair for my sister's sake. It was my sister, my mother, my father, and my husband against me, my young son, and my daughter. It was four people against a seven-month pregnant woman. I did not even have the strength to argue how wrong this was, or to ask what I had done for them to conspire against me at my time of need. I wished my son and daughter were old enough to speak for me, to defend me, but they were too little to even understand what was going on. My husband told me I either had to accept the choice presented to me or leave the house with my son and daughter. My parents also sided with my rich husband, so if I had not agreed to his order, I wouldn't have had anywhere to stay, not even at my parents' house.

That day, I left my husband, my parents, and my younger sister for good. I left the house with my children and travelled far away from our village. I did not have any friends or relatives who could help me. I know my parents and my husband expected me to stay out for one or two days and return to them, accepting their decision out of desperation. But I was determined to either live by myself or die rather than live that disgusting life. I loved my sister very much, after all, she's my baby sister. I was not ready to share my husband with her, so I left my husband with her fully.

I travelled far from the village to a town. At a construction site, I asked for a place to stay and for work. Those good people understood my situation, they saw I was pregnant and had two young children. They gave me a small place to sleep, offered me a job, and even helped me through my pregnancy. Soon enough, I delivered my third baby, it was a girl again, and I was happy. At the same time, I trembled with fear about how I would raise them. Once I started getting regular shifts at the building sites and was settling into my new life, I travelled back to my husband's town and initiated the divorce. I wanted the divorce to be my last gift to my sister, because only then could she marry him, right? After the divorce, I felt completely free. I worked very hard to educate my children. Life was hell; I spilt blood and sweat to educate and provide for them. In between my innocent children would ask me why I was not with their father. Those innocent questions filled me with shame and made me tear every single time. I am blessed with the best-behaved and understanding children in the world because as they grew up, they understood me and stopped asking that question.

It has been 37 years, and after so much struggle, my first daughter now works in HR at a company. I do not remember the name of the company, she keeps telling me many times, but I can't remember. She is happily married, and my youngest daughter also works in HR and is happily married. I heard from some neighbors back in the village that my sister and my ex-husband are happy together. They have children of their own and are well settled. I never remarried; I have been alone. Two girls and a boy, how would I have had time for another marriage? But I have my children. They are my world, and I'm happy with the life we have now.

You want to know about my son, don't you? My son's a chartered accountant. You know how hard it is to become a chartered accountant and how many exams they must write to become one. But he is not married yet. He loves a girl, but she is from another caste. I do not care about caste or religion. Years ago, when my three children and I took shelter in a building site with no money, all the Gods helped us. No one sent us away based on my caste or religion. So, I don't care about caste or religion; as long as the girl is true and takes good care of my boy, I'm okay with any caste or religion. But the girl is from a higher caste, and her parents are very rich. I tried many times, along with my boy, to speak to them, to accept the marriage, but they are too stubborn. They want to marry their daughter to a boy of the same caste and the same status.

With so much difficulty, I raised my three children. I taught them everything good, educated them well, and sometimes it breaks my heart to know that some people judge them by nothing more than their background. My boy has loved that girl for nearly seven years now, and she is very good and loves him so much. At this age, anybody is free to do anything, they do not need parents' permission anymore. But my boy convinced the girl to wait until her parents agreed to the marriage.

My boy believes they cannot live a happy life by hurting their parents. I know what my parents did to me - I know what my ex-husband did to me, but knowing how my boy lives and the principles he holds, I know I raised my boy well.

15 THE WIDOWED MOTHER

She had four beautiful children. Two of them were on her right, and the other two children were on the left of her when she was crying in front of her husband's lifeless body. Surrounded by relatives, she was beating her chest and crying uncontrollably as she was going through a rollercoaster of emotions. Although devastated, she was also confused as to why she was glad that her husband's pain was finally over and he was at peace. She was nervous because two of her children were only halfway through their long education, and she did not know how to help them finish. Rent was due in a few weeks, and the only job goer in the family was lying dead right in front of her.

Not only the only breadwinner, but the man of the house was also gone, and she was vulnerable now. She was trembling in fear, thinking who would support her, who would take advantage of her vulnerability now and most importantly, who would arrange the funeral formalities.

In her own words:

This was way back in 1997, and you could tell remarrying was not an option for us traditional and middle-class families. I had 4 children back then, and just that number should tell you how much my husband and I loved each other (laughs shyly)."

"Looking back, it was the worst time of our lives. My husband was lying dead in front of me, and I realized no one would call me Sumangali (woman blessed with a living husband) anymore. I can't have a head full of flowers and wear my kunkumam (sindhur) anymore. I hadn't even stepped out to buy vegetables. Even for shopping, I used to go with my husband. Now I had to work full-time for the first time in my life. What will I do? Who will take me for a job? Questions strangled me.

My husband's hospital bills were still unpaid. And even as we were mourning his death, people arrived with small chits in their hands, saying he had borrowed money from them and demanding we repay it. It felt like being kicked while we were already on the ground.

Luckily, my husband was the youngest of his 7 brothers and 1 sister. They supported us through the funeral and financially helped us. Days passed after the funeral, and I am still thankful to my relatives and my late husband's brothers, who helped us financially. But I did not want my children to be dependent on anyone. So, I quickly found a job. It was an odd manual job, but I had to take it. I was married at a very young age, and I had never worked before in my life. It was a bit difficult at first, but things gradually became more manageable, at least at work. Outside of that, life only became more challenging. I say this because we were a family of 5. I struggled to feed my family and educate my two children at the same time.

In between, there were other expenses: buying new clothes, stationery for school, school fees, uniform, etc. My children were still children at that stage. They didn't fully understand how dire our situation was. I budgeted every week with care, and when my children asked for new clothes, I had to say no most of the time, with a heavy heart. That was hard enough. But what truly shattered me was when they would sometimes ask for something nice to eat. Each time I had to refuse even a small treat; it broke me so deeply that I didn't always have the strength to answer. They would plead with me, their own mother, for a while, and when they realized I wasn't responding, they would quietly walk away. Then it would be my turn to fall apart, crying because I could not provide for my children. Having to refuse your child's simplest requests because of poverty is a kind of pain I would not wish on my worst enemy.

We are a god-fearing family, and I am very strict about sending prayers to our lord. But my husband's death, my hardships and our poverty - those prayers we sent to the lord seemed wasteful. At that time, I only wished a quick death for my children and me. I know it is not what a mother should say, but at that time, that was what was going through my mind to get away from this harsh world. It all seems like a bad dream now, and I have no idea how we overcame that phase of our lives. Within a few months of getting a job, two of my eldest sons also took responsibility and took the job they found at the time. With what little we earned, my daughter finished her studies, and I made my youngest son finish his. I guess it was the impact of his father's death because my youngest son excelled in his studies after that, both in school and in college. It was a proud moment for me when his photo was printed on the college banner alongside the top scorers. Two of my eldest sons worked really hard and are now settled in government jobs. We all live together. Isn't that any mother's dream? - To always have her children nearby and, at the same time, see them settling in life? My daughter has two beautiful children who are growing up well. My sons are married too, and my only wish is to see my youngest son get married soon. When that day comes, I will be at peace, knowing the responsibilities my husband left me are complete, and I can meet him in the afterlife without any guilt.

We used to live in an old, dark house, but by God's grace, we rebuilt it, and now we live comfortably, all as one family. I am grateful for what I have. It is not like we do not have struggles anymore. We still do have struggles, but everything is manageable now. All thanks to the strength I had in me when I was stripped away from everything.

No doubt that we went through so many hardships to get to where we are today. I was young and had the energy to work. I had good relatives who were kind enough to help us through our worst times. I just feel sorry for all the widowed mothers out there who have to fight their battles all alone and with bad relatives. God has answered my prayers now. Now my prayers are not for myself anymore - it's for all the widowed mothers out there getting ready to face an unfortunate, unexpected battle.

16 THE MOURNING WOMAN

Being a full-time teacher at a small-town school, her world revolved around just three people: her brother, mother, and dad. In that beautiful small world, there were just two problems - her mom had been bedridden for 6 years, and her dad was severely affected by diabetes, such that he had a rotting leg. Nevertheless, she cared for both of them without a problem for almost ten years, allowing them to reach their late 70s safely. During the years, her hard work for her family and her parents did not stop, but the struggles did increase as her parents grew older and more senile.

For a long time, her house became less a home and more a small sickroom. It always smelled of ointment and medicine. One day, her mom fell critically ill and was rushed to the hospital, where she was looked after for 3 weeks. Burdened with a new duty towards their mother, she and her brother shared the responsibility of staying with their mother in the hospital. Her brother worked night shifts, so he would arrive at the hospital to look after his mom during the day, and as she was a daytime school teacher, she would stay by her mother's side during the night. When it was morning, she cooked for her entire family, went back to work, and returned to the hospital to look after her mom again during the night. Sleep was out of the equation as hospitals for visitors aren't hotels that accommodate guests comfortably, and food for energy was of no interest due to too much stress and fear of what might happen to her mother.

As years pass, we live long enough to find out that we took care of our loved ones in the best way possible, only to realize later that life was waiting all along to take them away from us in the worst way possible. The same fate was waiting for her - at the end of the 3rd week, her mom was so ill that the doctors decided that it was best just to discharge her, and within days, her mother passed in her sleep.

Heartbroken, but not defeated, because she still had a sick father to take care of. As the woman of the house, she took responsibility for all household activities. But within 3 months, tragedy struck again, and her dad was hospitalized, and it was back to routine for her and her brother at the same hospital.

The same doctors who had lost hope in her mother previously, now lost hope in her father and discharged him too, stating that it's better if he stayed with his family during his last few days. At this point, history was repeating itself for her as, within a week, her dad too left her to join his wife in eternity.

Within days after the demise of both her parents, the house did not smell like medicine anymore, but that only made her miss her parents even more. Unburdened by the years of responsibility which lay on her shoulders, she now had all the time in the world, but the woman who knew how to take care of her parents forgot how to take care of herself.

The sorrow of losing both their parents in just three months made her brother look for solace in alcohol. Of course, being a man, it was easier for him as alcohol was socially accessible to him. But unlike her brother, being a woman, liquor was not easily and socially accessible for her, so there was nothing to numb her pain. Heartbreak without alcohol is brutal. It is like a pain without painkillers - nothing skipped, every inch felt. She spent most of her days indoors, crying and praying and reliving the memories she had with her parents. She looked for refuge in God and her friends. She knew alcohol would not help her with her pain, but she believed praying to God would at least give her parents peace for their souls.

Her brother had friends to talk to and stayed out late. But it was not safe for her to do so, and she didn't have the same generation of friends who advised her or joined her in booze. Sore throat and teary eyes were what she experienced after the demise of her parents. Lucky for her, she had good friends whom she could rely on to speak to. As days passed, she hurt less, and her relatives found her a good groom in just

1 year after the death of her parents. As of 2026, she is now happily married in Paris and spends most of her time playing with her beautiful 2-year-old daughter. She believes her own mom has returned to her in the form of her 2-year-old daughter. She eagerly wishes to welcome her father, too, in the form of a future son.

17 THE ACCIDENTAL HERO

A seven-year-old girl was crying along with her five-year-old brother. They didn't even know why they were crying. At that age, they just went with the energy in the house. Their mother lay dead in front of them, and the sound of crying echoed through every room, so the little girl and her brother cried too.

God looked down and asked, out of curiosity, "Why are those children crying?"

An angel replied, "They're crying because their mother just died."

God said, "That is unfortunate, but not to worry. Their father will take care of them."

The angel paused. "Uma. No. They are alone. It is complicated."

God frowned. "Then send one of our angels."

The angel shook their head. "You know it doesn't work like that."

God nodded slowly and thought for a moment. "Fine. Who is the next of kin?"

"There's an aging grandmother," the angel said. "She is fifty-two years old. She is tired. But she is still standing."

God said, "Good. Then make her their angel."

And so, it was done.

I was that little girl who lost her mother. I'm all grown up now, but whenever I think about my childhood, how suddenly it turned tragic, and how I was saved by my grandma, I picture this conversation happening between God and his angels.

My grandma never planned to rescue anyone. She did not sign up to raise children again. But when my brother and I needed someone, and the world looked away even with plenty of people around, she stepped in. And this is how her story begins.

She was born into poverty, in a time when girls were allowed only a small slice of education and then pushed into duty. She studied until the fifth standard because that was all she was "permitted." Her childhood was simple, until the day life took something right in front of her eyes.

My grandma was still very young, pregnant with my mother. Her baby shower was just two days away. That day, her own mother, my great-grandmother, was serving her food. One spoon of rice fell onto my grandma's plate, and before the second spoon could be served, her mother collapsed and died.

No warning. No last words. One moment alive; the next, gone.

Her mother's heart stopped, but the shock and grief kept moving, straight into my grandma. Death can be cruel often: if it is not you crying, it is someone else crying for you. Pain does not vanish; it changes hands. Generation after generation.

Pregnancies are supposed to be a happy season in a woman's life. My grandma had pictured her mother holding the baby, rocking her, laughing at her small sounds. Instead, she watched those hands go still and cold. Years later, she still says that whenever she sits down to eat, the memory returns, the plate, the spoon, the falling. She calls it a curse. Sometimes I think life curses us for sins we never committed. While I may not know much about curses, I do know about trauma. One moment could stain a lifetime.

That was the first station in her long train of sorrows. Her baby shower was cancelled. But she kept going. Twenty-two days after her own mother died, my grandma gave birth to my mother.

A woman could have achieved a hundred things before, but after childbirth, one look at her baby makes it feel like that is her greatest achievement of all. My grandma felt that joy too, but it was weighed down by the grief of her mother not being there to witness it. Still, she raised my mother with a determination that did not ask permission.

My grandma was still recovering from her mother's death, and for a while she let herself enjoy the early days of motherhood with my mother. But life did not let her stay happy for long. Typhoid came for my mother when she was only seven. Back then, our town was still a village, and real treatment was far away. People told my grandma plainly: if my mother stayed there, she would not survive. So, my grandma sent her to relatives in the city. Hospitals were nearby there. Medicines existed. They saved her life.

But the fear stayed. What if it happened again? Everyone told my grandma to keep my mother in the city, close to hospitals and doctors. My grandma had no choice but to agree, even though it meant distance. With a heavy heart, she left her seven-year-old in the city, away from home, but closer to safety. They met whenever they could. Love learned to travel.

Later, my grandma married my mother to my father.

Then I was born.

For a while, life looked calmer, like maybe the worst had already happened.

Then, when I was seven, my mother died.

The ambulance came. My brother and I ran toward her body. I was seven. He was five. We did not understand death. We only understood that something had been taken, and that our crying couldn't bring it back.

That was when my grandma became our angel.

My grandma often said, "Your mother was seven when I had to send her away to the city. And you were seven too when she handed you over to me and left permanently. Maybe she wanted to compensate for the years I lost with her, by giving me you."

My grandma brought us to her village. She was fifty-two, an age people called "resting age." Instead, responsibility tightened around her: school, money, food, safety, the future. Even as a child, I remembered her crying hard at nights, not only because her daughter had died, but because two children had been left behind and she had no map for raising them.

But her tears at night always followed with mornings determined with plans and actions. Not big speeches, just lists in her head, quiet decisions, small sacrifices stacked one on top of another. If she had to borrow, she borrowed. If she had to walk farther for cheaper groceries, she walked. If she had to swallow pride to ask someone for help, she swallowed it. She did all of it with a face that tried to look normal, because children noticed panic even when you hid it.

She enrolled my brother in a private school. She did not have the money, but she had the intention. For me, she chose a public school. At that time, many women around her believed the boy would earn and the girl would marry early. I'm not defending that thinking, only saying this: my grandma did what she believed was best for me, with the knowledge she had and in the world, she was raised in. I also remember what it felt like: I envied my brother's English books while I studied in my mother tongue.

Still, she fought to educate us both. She lived off pension money and did side work whenever she could, cooking, cleaning, going to the fields for daily wages. And even while she worried about survival, she didn't steal my childhood. She used to give me a lot of money for samosas, mango slices with salt and chili, chocolates, small joys that told me life could still be sweet for a child who grew up without a mother.

When I became a teenager, some relatives treated me unfairly. They gave me chores not out of need, but out of power, because who would stand up for a motherless girl?

My grandma did.

She fought for me, loudly if she had to. She told them to do their own work. She didn't let my quietness become an invitation. Sometimes she stood between me and the shouting, small 4-foot 6-inch body, big voice, like a wall. Later she would come to me and act casual, offer me fruit, tell me jokes, so I didn't carry the heaviness all day.

She pampered me so much. Most girls in my village learned cooking early. I didn't, not because I was special, but because she refused to make my life feel like punishment. She wanted me to study, to grow, to breathe.

Parent-teacher meetings were a comedy because of her. I was a below-average student, and once during the meeting, a teacher complained that I wasn't attentive and my marks were poor. I expected scolding. Instead, my grandmother defended me loudly like a lawyer in front of other my other classmates and their parents:

"What are you saying, teacher? You're mistaken. She studies all night long!"

My classmates heard it. The next day they teased me, "Yes yes, she studies all night… that's why she's first rank!", and even now, it makes me laugh. But what stays with me is this: she defended me without hesitation. She protected my dignity even when my marks didn't.

As I grew older, I asked her again and again why my brother got private school and I didn't. She never said, "Because you are a girl." But I could see the guilt in her face.

She learned fast. She watched the world changing and realised girls needed education just as much. When relatives started saying, "Now is the right age, marry her," she stood like iron and said no.

She made me continue my studies. And after school, she insisted I join a good private college. The fees were expensive, but this was her way of fixing what she couldn't fix earlier, giving me a door she had once been able to open only for my brother.

I chose mathematics and became a maths graduate. I am a bit embarrassed to admit it, but as a maths graduate, even I need a calculator for big additions and subtractions. My grandmother, with only fifth-standard schooling, can do calculations instantly, as if numbers obey her. When shopkeepers tried to confuse her, she corrected them on the spot. Sometimes I thought: if she had been given my education, she would have gone so far.

After graduation, I found a job in my town. Some days my shift started at 6 a.m., which meant waking up at 5 to catch the bus.

My grandmother woke up with me.

Not because I asked, because she couldn't bear the thought of me leaving while she slept. She moved quietly, as if her comfort might make me feel alone. She made hot tea every morning, without fail, then stood nearby while I got ready, pretending she was busy so I wouldn't notice she was watching me like a mother watched a child cross a road.

Sometimes, because I was in a hurry, I would miss the tea my grandma prepared for me. Then, while I waited for my bus at the bus stop, I would see her running toward me with that tea glass in her hand, running so carefully that not a single drop spilled. The whole bus stop would stare at us. I felt embarrassed.

She didn't care.

She would make me drink it right there, from that big silver glass, like it was the most normal thing in the world. For her, I should never leave the house with an empty stomach, not even once. And if she had to run through the street to make sure of it, then she would.

When I started earning, I tried to give her the joys she never had time for. New sarees. A restaurant meal. She used to believe restaurants were for rich people; with me, she walked in like she belonged, because she trusted her granddaughter would handle everything.

Our whole life, we lived in a town that had five beaches. Yet she had never gone to the sea, not once. Responsibility had been her ocean. So one day I took her to the shore, and then onto a boat. She enjoyed being there and laughed like a child.

I took her to the mall too. She stared at the lights and floors like she had entered a palace. The escalator frightened her. She hesitated at the edge while a line built behind us and my heart raced with embarrassment. Then she squeezed my hand and stepped on anyway, trusting me more than she feared it.

Even after I started earning, she didn't truly rest. She kept preparing for the next milestone. She saved every rupee I gave her. When my wedding came, her pension might have been enough for the jewelry she wanted to buy me, but she still did odd jobs when she could. She wanted to give me more than "enough." She wanted me to feel chosen.

I married a good man. He understood my grandma wasn't "extra baggage." She was the reason I stood where I stood. So, we took her with us whenever we could, and it took her seventy years to finally step outside her hometown and see places she never imagined.

My grandmother had one dream she repeated like a prayer: she wanted to fly.

Many of our relatives worked in airports, and she used to complain, "They all work in airports, but they never take me inside." She didn't see it as an office where my relatives work. She saw it as a wonder.

When my husband and I got a visa to work abroad, we took her to the airport. She walked inside and lit up like a child. She wasn't sad that I was leaving; she was proud, proud that the granddaughter people once told to stop studying and marry young had taken her into a world, she thought she would never touch.

I had a list of things I wanted to do for her. I had done almost everything on it, except one: taking her onto an airplane. I am not sure when I can fulfill this dream for my grandma.

Sometimes doubt swirls in me, tickets, limited leave from work, passport paperwork, time. It all feels too heavy to fit into one plan. But then I remind myself who I came from. I am my grandma's granddaughter. The same blood ran in me. If she could raise two children after fifty-two with nothing but pension money and will, surely, I could find a way to give her this last dream.

When people hear this story of hers, they might shrug and say, She did what any responsible woman would do.

But they don't know how many times life came back to take more from her. My grandma is truly a legend for putting up a fight with fate itself.

My younger brother, the five-year-old who cried beside me in front of our mother's body, grew up, studied, and graduated college. We thought the storm had finally loosened its grip.

Then he died.

Life took him away in one moment. My grandma had poured love into him for years, and then she had to bury him, too. I was my brother's sister. I loved him so much, but love was the only thing I gave him.But my grandma, she gave him everything, from the nothing she had. She fed him first. She worried for him the loudest. She carried his needs like they were her own.

Grief broke her differently when he was gone. But she did not fall, because I was still alive. Someone still needed her. So, she stayed standing.

And tragedy did not just stop with us.

My grandmother's other granddaughter, my cousin, faced her own nightmare. Her husband fell into a coma just a month before she gave birth. Overnight, their home lost its "man of the house," and they were left holding everything at once: a newborn who could not wait, and a business that couldn't pause.

That was when my seventy-four-year-old grandma stepped in, not as a visitor, not as a helper, but as a mother. She held the baby. She handled the accounts. She did that quick, fearless math of hers while the rest of the house shook with worry. She showed up the way she always did, without waiting to be asked.

Just when she should have been allowed to rest, life pulled her back into duty. That was who she had always been: an accidental hero.

The last time I saw my grandma was at the airport.

She stood there after sending me off, small, steady, watching until I disappeared past the gate. For a long time, I imagined she went home and finally rested.

But that was not how her story worked.

From the airport, she went straight into my cousin's home. She took my cousin's newborn into her arms and began doing what she had done her whole life: keeping a family alive. She balanced the business books, planned feedings and naps, and carried the days forward with her quiet discipline.

And I carried one promise inside me like a prayer: one day, I would bring her onto an airplane. Not just to an airport, but into the sky.

Because if a four-foot-six woman could stand tall through everything life threw at us, and hold up three generations with nothing but love and will, then surely, I, her granddaughter, could make that one last dream of here is to come true.

She is my accidental hero.

And I want to see her again, standing there with the same calm eyes, with that big silver glass of tea, asking if I had eaten well. When I go back, I want to hold her hands and tell her the truth: she had not just raised children. She had kept an entire family alive.

This is her story, the rest of what is left of my family is here because she refused to give up.

18 THE OLD WOMAN

I was born in 1936, when our village had no electricity, and India had no freedom. I have seen the flag change, the borders tear, leaders fall, and still the sun rise on our little fields. I was born poor. I lost my mother early. My father married again, and we got a stepmother. Our stepmother had children of her own with my father soon, and she fed them alone and often left us starving. She educated her children and made us work in the fields.

When I came of age, I was married to a good man, but as his second wife. My husband's first wife had died and left two daughters. My husband, at the time, was an active-duty military man, and his job often sent him away from us for months at a time. He left his two girls under my care whenever he went away. I looked at those small, motherless faces and swore I would never be to them what my stepmother was to me. I cooked for them, fed them, and educated them, but they did not accept me. Sometimes, love is a seed, and sometimes it falls on a rock. Nevertheless, stepmother or birth mother, I was still their mother, so I took good care of them, and I can proudly say it when I meet my lord when my time comes.

I was born in a small hut, but I married someone who had a sheet house, which was a little bit bigger than the one I was born in, so I felt like it was an upgrade for me. I had two daughters. The first was healthy. The second, unfortunately, came fragile and disabled. The doctors said no matter how old she gets; she cannot talk and would only have the brain of a five-year-old. People told me to put my disabled, mute daughter in a home where she would be somebody else's problem, but I did not do such a thing. She is mine. What is given to you by God is not to be returned. I will take care of everything that God has given to me until I die.

In our village, girls were married young and sent to the fields, not to school. But in my childhood, my mother fought for our education. She never let us skip a day. Even now, I can recognize English letters, even in long, complicated words, I can say the letters clearly, but I can't read the words. I learned the alphabet, not the language. And when my mother died and a stepmother entered our home, my schooling ended.

I wanted to be different. I wanted all my daughters, both stepdaughters and my real daughters, to be learned but my stepdaughters were not interested in education, and they married early and left the house. My second daughter was disabled, so we always kept her with us at home. But we sent my first daughter to her aunt in town to study. Education in towns was costly. Money was tight, but we managed to send it to her aunt every month to provide her with food and education. When my first daughter was old enough, she married a decent man in the same town where she had studied. They struggled financially but managed. Later, she had two sons. We travelled every year, me, my husband, and our disabled daughter, to see those beautiful boys in town. The roads were long, the buses crowded, but my heart swelled every time those little hands held my cheeks.

Just a few years later, my husband died. The small house we lived in felt bigger after his demise. After his death, it was only my disabled girl now in that house in that village. I was afraid, but his army pension kept us surviving, rice on the plate, oil for the lamp, and that money also helped me send a little to my first daughter to set aside for my grandchildren's education. And then another blow: the land. We lived on the plot in my husband's name. His first wife's daughters claimed their share. I would not deny anyone what is theirs - after all, they are his daughters. So, I sold the land quickly as they demanded, paid them their share. Today, that land is worth crores. What did I sell it for? Do not ask. A woman who is alone pays the lowest price and the highest cost.

After we sold the only place my disabled daughter and I could call home, we rented a small house in the same village. I wrote to my daughter: I have sold the land, given the shares, and kept yours safe. She is soft-hearted, cannot bear her people to suffer. She begged her husband to take us into their house. He is a good man, and he agreed. We moved to the town. The old dream my husband and I whispered ten years ago came true: near my daughter, near my grandsons - if only my husband were alive to see all this.

After my husband's death, those days with my daughters and grandchildren always around me healed me. I would walk the boys to the bus stop, fan them when the power cut came, and warm milk at night. They slept like angels, mouths open, a foot always pushed out from the sheet. Then they became teenagers, angels with elbows. The elder one, my favorite, grew sharp, but sometimes the words he spoke pierced. Not because he was bad, because he was young. Once, I would have cut people out of my life for just a wrong look. Now I have outlived my anger. Someone my age who is too old to be tired, their heart only gives and forgives. My grandchildren grew up fast, finished school and went to college in a different city. My daughter's family climbed from the lower middle class to the upper middle class. Still, it was not enough for college fees. My pension rose a little; I gave it gladly, food, notebooks, exam forms. The boys graduated. They work now. I have carried much pain: my mother's death, my husband's, my second daughter's disability, the stepdaughters' coldness, and my own grandson's rudeness. I kept nothing for myself. Everything I have belongs to my daughter and my grandchildren. Some days I think: if they told me to leave, where would I take my disabled child? I was once strong and independent, but years of being dependent have made me forget how to be independent.

My grandchildren did many good things for me. They bought me new bed and new clothes, and pressed money into my palm, though I saved it back only for them. They built a house, a bungalow, I call it, and gave me a room of my own, with a fan and a water heater and a window that breathes. I am grateful. But what I really want is their time. I have so many stories to tell, experiences to share, but nobody has time for this old lady. There was a time when someone saw me in a new sari and said, "Beautiful." Now my daughter gets me new clothes now and then, but nobody compliments me. It has been years since I received a compliment. If only I could get my youth back.

From her grandson:

I am her eldest grandson, and I live abroad now. The news of my grandmother's passing hit me like thunder. I flew home at once to pay my last respects to my grandmother. She died in 2023. I still remember that night. After a tiring 1.5-day travel back to India, I just kept staring at my grandmother's lifeless body. I loved her deeply, and she loved me even more, yet I could not cry. My eyes were pained, and my throat hurt, but not a single drop of tear came out. Perhaps that was my punishment: to hold the pain inside and not let it go, for the careless teenage words that once made her weep.

Everything we are today carries her handprint. The land we live in was bought with her pension money. She partly funded our education, and the life we have is also through her. She could have stayed in her village, lived on the pension, and kept her door shut. Instead, she fed us, funded us, forgave us and loved us till her last breath. She was bedridden for nine months. My mother told me that my grandmother often asked for me: When will he come?' But I did not make it in time.

At the funeral, I did what a first grandson must. I shouldered the casket until the weight pained my bones. I lowered her into the ground. I stayed last at the grave. Still, the tears did not come.

The next morning after my grandmother's burial, I found my mother crying alone. She feared the same thing her mother once feared: How will I take care of my disabled sister? After all, my mother is the strong granddaughter of my grandmother. I said she would find a way. My mother recalled her childhood days with my grandmother in their village. She remembered the state they were in. My mother said something I will not forget: "She was born in a hut. But she left this earth from a bungalow."

It is true. But the bungalow is not the point. The point is the path between the hut and the bungalow, built with this woman's sacrifices: the portion she didn't eat, the coin she saved, the bus she took, the land she sold, the grudge she didn't keep, the child she refused to give away, the boys she forgave until they became men.

If I could have one more hour, I would sit on the floor by her cot, take her warm, wrinkled hand, and say the word she waited to hear in every new sari: "Beautiful."

Since I cannot, I will try to live a life that says it for me: to show up, to listen, to feed, to forgive. To hold my people close while they are still here. This is what my grandmother has taught me through her kind and simple life. Huts and bungalows are made of brick and money. But families, families are built of women like her.

19 THE TRANSWOMAN

"Lights, camera… action!"

The cameras start rolling.

The crew doesn't fidget. No one chats. Everyone is locked in, listening to her like the room itself has agreed to stay still. She is not acting. She is telling her life into the lens, calm, simple, honest. No fear. No ego. Just truth, spoken like it's finally allowed to exist out loud.

When she finishes the scene, the director calls, "Cut!", and you can hear the joy in her voice.

For a second, the room stays quiet. Then the crew breaks into applause. Cheers like they've been holding it in. She steps off set, speaks briefly with the director, thanks her, shakes a few hands, and then it's my turn.

Me: Thank you for agreeing to share your story.

Her: Thank you for having me. So, what do you want to know about me?

Me: Can we start from your childhood?

Her: Sure.

"I was born in 1991. A normal birth, a normal family, except it is that kind of 'normal' where people still counted grandsons like medals. My parents were very proud when I was born. They announced the news to everyone. They feasted. Everyone was happy."

She pauses, then says it plainly.

"I was eleven when I knew I was a girl."

Not think. No wonder. I knew I was a girl.

"I knew it in the way I sat, the way I spoke, the way I felt inside. I was a girl… trapped in a boy's body."

"My parents tried to correct me. They taught me how a "son" should talk, laugh, sit, live. They tried to train me into boyhood as if it were a skill I could learn."

"I tried to obey them. I really tried. But how do you behave like something you are not? A boy is a boy. A girl is a girl. Children do not 'act' gender. They just are. For most people, school is the golden part of life. For me, it is a long sadness. They say kids do not see differences. That they just befriend anyone. That did not happen for me, sadly. The girls said I was pretending to be a girl, so they avoided me. The boys said I was strange for acting like a girl, so they avoided me, too."

"You know how kids love to take unnecessary restroom breaks just to kill time in class? I never did that. In school, I stopped using the restroom during breaks, not because I did not need to go, but because fear became stronger than the body."

"I had to use the boys' restroom because I had no choice. "And I can't explain the horror of looking at parts that feel like someone else's."

"People joke, 'I wish I could try the opposite gender for one day.' They can try a piece of it right now. Step outside dressed as the 'other' gender for one afternoon and count the stares. Even if nobody says anything, feel that knot inside, the discomfort, the nerves, the voice saying, this is not me. That feeling is my every day."

"A child would only want three things: friends, toys, and clothes."

"Friends, I had almost none. You already know why.

"Toys, I wanted teddy bears, Barbie dolls, pink toys. Instead, I got trucks and action figures. I did not even know what to do with them.

"Clothes, I longed for tops, skirts, sarees. I got shirts, shorts, and trousers. Every morning felt like wearing someone else's skin. Even the joy of receiving new clothes was not there for me when I was a kid."

"I'm like other girls. I love clothes. I love looking good. But the clothes I was given were the wrong type, the wrong color, for the wrong gender."

"So that's my childhood."

Me: How was life after school?

Her: I thought college would be kinder to me. Very soon, I learn it wasn't.

"In school, I told myself that kids are immature. That is why they mocked me. That is why they gave me names. But college was worse in a different way. The 'mature' ones judged me. Some avoided me. Some pitied me. And the worst of all, some used me."

"But in college, I found it easier to speak to girls. Boys stayed at a distance."

"Like any other girl, I wanted to talk to the handsome boys in college. I wanted to feel normal. But I was terrified. Back then, I was still living in a male body. Who would speak to me without making it a joke, without making it hurt?"

Me: What did you do after graduating?

Her: I finished my degree. I found a coder's job at a publishing house. And for one small season… I breathed normally.

She smiled when she said that line, like she was remembering what peace felt like.

Me: When did you transition? And what was it like?

Her: When I was finally old enough, it was my body, my rules.

"I could legally transition after I was no longer a minor, but my parents said a strict no". "Multiple times" "in multiple ways." "Before I realized it, I was kicked out of the house."

"I knew the job will also disappear the moment I transitioned. I knew I would lose stability, safety, everything that looks like "normal."

And still,

"I choose to transition."

"The surgery cost Rs. 50,000 back then. I did not have that money. But I still chose to do it by getting loans. And after transitioning, I was bedridden for thirty days like any other transgender who first got her surgery."

Me: If you were kicked out, did not have a job, then who took care of you?

Her: Once my parents let me go, someone else adopted me.

"I reached out, hesitating, scared, to the trans people in my town."

"To my surprise, they were kind. They supported me without asking for anything in return. I had no background, no money, and no future. They knew I might be a burden, and still, they took me in."

She admits she expected rejection.

"When you try telling your friend you want to start a business same as theirs, you can watch their face change. A friend can become cautious in a second, because suddenly your competition. I expected that look from them too. But they did not flinch. They made room."

"Even with almost nothing, they chose to help."

Me: How was recovery for you after your transition? What did you go through? Her: People say a mother's labor is a rebirth. Believe them. But for many of us, transitioning is also a rebirth.

"It is pain. It is a slow hour. It is fear. After surgery, I was bedridden for nearly a month. The ones who bathed me, fed me, changed my sheets, stayed up through fever nights, were trans women."

"I had no home, no job, no money. They took me in and asked for nothing. I really wish that people would remember this when they speak about 'people like us.' Kindness lives here too."

Me: How does the future look for trans women?

Her: The world is changing. Slowly. But it is changing.

"After surgery, I lost more than blood. I lost my job. I lost my home. I lost so much. I did what too many of us are pushed to do, I begged on the streets. Survival is not glamorous. It is heat, dust, rain, and frequent humiliations that you swallow because there is no other way to eat."

"When I was a kid, things were different. I did not get accepted by my own parents nor the people around me."

"But I see parents who accept their children now. I see trans people studying, working, and leading. I see people today are kinder towards us. I see doors opening, but not enough."

"I also see films that preach awareness, but cast men to play us, or give trans roles to non-trans and beautiful-looking women. I do not have anything against those actors. But if a film wants to teach 'awareness,' it should practice it too. If the story is about a trans woman, hire a trans actress"

"Work matters. Dignity matters. I request that those in power not crush us, and then complain that we beg. Give opportunities so we can earn, so we can pay taxes, so we can live like citizens, be a part of your society, not like burdens."

Me: What does love look like for trans women?

Her: Honestly? We are among the least chosen.

"Even when we are chosen, it is often in secret. Some men come to 'explore,' then remember their families and neighbors suddenly, and leave."

"And they use the word 'love' while they do it."

"I do not hate men. All trans women are raised as boys first. Maybe that is why when we love, we love fiercely. We love steadily."

"In five years, I buried thirteen of my own sisters, trans women who can't bear it after being left."

"And when you have no job, no family, no friends… and then no love, what is left to hold on to?"

"Every time my phone rings at night, and it's one of my trans friends, my heart drops. I pick up hoping it is nothing, hoping it's just a normal call. But too often it is not. Someone has drunk poison. Someone is fighting for their life in a hospital. I wish this would stop."

"I am a learned person; I know research shows suicide risk is extremely high among transgender people, and that we face much higher rates of suicidal thoughts and attempts than the general population. It's hard to prove "the highest," because official statistics rarely track us properly. But the grief is real, and the losses are real."

"We are not asking for pity. We are asking for space."

"When a child runs, you do not tie their legs. That energy is childhood. In the same way, our femininity is not a performance to be punished. It is a truth to be protected."

"I wish I were exactly like other girls. I wish I could bleed, carry life, give birth. I will not. Maybe in another birth, the body meant for me will find me."

"Until then, I stand here as I am, asking to belong."

Me: "I understand the trans community faces so many challenges. But why transition if this life brings more negatives than positives? Why go through it if you might even lose your family?"

Her: "I wish it were easy to explain why we still do it, even when we know we might lose everything else."

"Imagine a child who chooses a life their parents never planned for them. A different career. A different path. Something their family doesn't approve of. That child still chooses it, not because the parents matter less, but because their life is theirs to live. They keep hoping that one day, when the parents see them standing on their own feet, acceptance will come."

She looks at me, steady.

"But gender isn't a job you leave at 6 p.m."

"How many of you work a job you hate? It's only eight hours a day, and still, it drains you, doesn't it? So many people realize they chose the wrong career. Years pass, experience piles up, and switching starts to feel impossible, so most people stay, even when they are unhappy. But the ones who do take the leap are never told they are immoral for choosing a life that fits them better.

If changing careers is not wrong, then changing gender isn't wrong either. And the truth is, we never chose the gender we were assigned at birth.

Now imagine living in a body that feels wrong, twenty-four hours a day. Every day. All year. All life. You do not get a break from it. You do not get to 'log out.'"

"Of course, some people do not transition. I know transwomen who never did because their parents did not allow it. Some marry. Some have children. They are living, but if you look into their eyes, it's like they left themselves behind a long time ago. They function. They survive. But inside, they are not alive the way they could have been."

"And if you've ever mastered something you never wanted, if you've ever lived a life that looks 'successful' from outside but feels like a prison inside, you already understand a part of my pain."

"Transition is not about hurting anyone. It's not about attention. It is not about rebellion. It is about being able to breathe in your own skin."

"We do so much just to be seen as who we are. People think transition is one surgery and it is done. It is not. For many of us, it is a long, expensive process, hormones, facial hair removal, voice training, sometimes surgeries. Some choose genital surgery, some do not. Some want facial surgery, some do not. But almost everyone is fighting something: a beard shadow, a voice that gets you stared at, a body shape the world refuses to read as female."

"And even after all that, the world still finds reasons to say, 'You're not enough.'"

"But we do it anyway. Not because it is easy. Because the alternative is harder: living every day as someone you are not."

"We do all these just to feel like we're living our dream. We are not hurting anyone. Not even sentimentally. We are merely doing all of these for ourselves."

Me: "What's your plan now in life?"

Her: I just finished acting in a documentary. I am thankful to my director.

She smiles, almost shyly.

"I do not have much talent. I do not have many skills. But I have one thing: character."

"Some transgender people you see on the street can be aggressive when they ask for money. I cannot stand that behavior. I also ask people for money, but I do it respectfully. And when someone says they do not have any, I bless them anyway. Not everyone is rich. Everyone carries a burden they may not be able to explain, and the last thing they need is for someone like me to take even the little they have.

"My director visited India from Germany and met me by coincidence during a moment like that. While other transgenders were being rude to tourists and locals, she noticed my politeness. She asked me to be part of the documentary she was making. I said yes, and now my film is going to film festivals in Europe, all thanks to her."

"I watched her direct the whole movie. And somehow, her love for direction transferred to me."

Now I am saving money. Gathering stories. Finding actors.

"And I plan to start my own YouTube channel to make short films. Real stories. And I want to earn through that, and I also want to spread awareness."

"I want to be seen as more than a lesson. More than a headline. More than a problem."

"As a woman."

20 TO YOU, THE GIRL WHO READS THIS

When this book first began as a project, countless people came forward and shared extraordinary stories, real histories. Both women and grown men told me what they, and their mothers, grandmothers, great-grandmothers, sisters, colleagues, and friends, had endured to bring their families to the stable place they are in now. They shared everything with eyes filling with tears and voices breaking with emotion.

Listening to them, I kept thinking the same thing: how little we realize that the good, stable families we see today were often held together by women, women who stood like pillars in the harshest storms.

Many of the people who trusted me with their heroes' stories felt relieved to finally say them out loud. Others spoke with hesitation. And a handful told me their stories weren't worth writing, and wouldn't be worth reading. They said only successful people deserve to have their lives written down.

That alone was confusing for me. Are the women in these stories not successful?

Does a woman who raised a champion have no part in that championship? If only the person who crosses the finish line deserves recognition, then we don't need teachers, trainers, coaches, or mentors.

The day you start admiring only tall, strong trees and forget the hands that planted them, without ever expecting recognition, you'll start to notice the forest shrinking and its trees rotting.

No one is a fortune teller. Most people live with a small, stubborn hope, that one day they will win, that one day their family will be safer, steadier, better than before. And even when people couldn't tell their stories perfectly, when emotions broke their sentences and grief interrupted their memories, the truth was still there. And that's why these stories are here.

When people talk about achievement, they usually point at famous names. They talk about awards, headlines, trophies, proof that can be seen by strangers.

But most women don't live their lives in public.

Most women build their greatest victories quietly, inside homes, inside grief, inside responsibilities, inside bodies that keep going even when the heart and mind is tired and exhausted.

And that is exactly why so many women forget they are achievers.

Because if achievements are rewarded only with fame and awards, then the unwritten stories go unnoticed. Histories and family legacies go unappreciated. Whole lives get reduced to "ordinary," when they were anything but.

So, let's ask the question properly:

What is achievement?

It is not only a moment on a stage. Sometimes it is the day you finally stand on your own feet.

A girl who grows up without a house, and later buys an apartment with her own money, even if it takes a loan, so her parents can finally live with security. That is achievement. It is not just a flat.

It is a lifetime of instability ending because you refused to repeat the past.

And sometimes achievement is not money, it is freedom.

A girl who is not allowed to go out without supervision, who later steps out on her own, learns the world, travels, makes videos, documents her life, and builds confidence one step at a time. That is achievement. Because freedom is not given to every girl the same way, it is earned, and sometimes it is fought for quietly, inside the same house that claims to love you.

Sometimes achievement doesn't look like gaining something.

Sometimes it looks like surviving something.

A woman loses both parents within a short time and still finds the strength to keep living, keep working, keep loving, keep building a future for herself. That is achievement. Because grief can turn a home into a graveyard, and yet she chooses to keep breathing inside it.

And sometimes achievement begins with the world trying to shrink you.

A woman is told, "You are poor, what confidence do you have to get pregnant?" as if motherhood belongs only to the privileged. And still she carries life, still she gives birth, still she raises that child with dignity, proving that love is not a luxury product. That is achievement.

Some achievements are quieter, almost invisible, until you understand what they cost.

A woman who was almost aborted, who was nearly erased before she even entered the world, grows up and becomes independent enough to care for her senile parents. The same life that was once treated as "optional" becomes the pillar holding two elders steady. That is achievement.

And sometimes achievement is motherhood, not the romantic version, but the real one.

An uneducated mother gives her children the education she never received. A new mother who doubts herself in a competitive world still raises a child who grows into stability and competence. A woman told she cannot have babies adopts a child and gives them safety, education, and love. A widowed mother loses her husband young, yet still educates her children, raises them, protects them, and gets them settled, carrying two roles in one life without ever being allowed to collapse.

That is achievement.

And sometimes achievement is rebuilding yourself.

A woman leaves a marriage that breaks her, then starts again, this time with wisdom, boundaries, and peace. A newlywed who is put down for everything slowly earns dignity in that house, earns her voice, earns respect, not by becoming cruel, but by becoming unshakeable. A girl who teaches others, lifts others, guides friends into good lives, and still builds her own life with them. That is achievement too.

And yes, sometimes achievement is simply being yourself.

A woman born in a man's body transitions. She loses comfort, loses acceptance, faces struggle, faces loneliness, yet still chooses honesty over hiding, and builds a life with dignity. That is achievement. Because living truthfully is not easy in a world that rewards pretending.

So no, achievement is not only something that gets applauded.

Some achievements don't get awards. They get scars. They get tired eyes. They get silent endurance. They get a woman who continues anyway.

And if you've done that, even once, then you have achieved something real.

Here is what you need to carry when you close this book:

Do not shrink your life just because it isn't famous.

Do not call your victories "small" just because they weren't celebrated.

Do not doubt your worth just because nobody announced your progress.

Some of the strongest things a woman can do,

she will do alone. Quietly. Without witnesses.

And that does not make it less valuable.

It makes it truer.

So, if the world forgets to clap, clap for yourself.

If the world forgets to name your strength, name it yourself.

If the world forgets to see you, learn to see yourself, clearly, fully, without apology.

And then do something even bigger:

Look at another woman's quiet life, the one that looks "normal" from the outside, and say the words this world withholds too easily:

"I see you."

Because the moment women start recognizing each other's unseen victories, we stop measuring life by fame. We start measuring it by truth.

And truth is what you have carried all along.

You matter.

Not because you are famous.

Because you are real.

ABOUT THE AUTHOR

Erasto Philippe is a UK-based Non-Resident **Indian** author whose work is shaped by years of listening closely to real lives, especially the lives of women who carry silent battles with steady faces. A graduate of the **University of Greenwich, London**, he has built his career in the UK while also mentoring Indian students through their most fragile transitions: finishing their studies, navigating uncertainty, finding work, and learning to stand on their own feet.

You, The Girl Who Reads This was born from that world of conversations, letters written not to instruct, but to accompany. With warmth, clarity, and respect, he writes to women at life's thresholds, grief and recovery, marriage and divorce, motherhood and loss, work, and identity, reminding the reader that survival is already a form of victory.

www.ingramcontent.com/pod-product-compliance
Ingram Content Group UK Ltd.
Pitfield, Milton Keynes, MK11 3LW, UK
UKHW021408190726
13845UKWH00028B/955